Communications in Computer and Information Science 959

Commenced Publication in 2007
Founding and Former Series Editors:
Phoebe Chen, Alfredo Cuzzocrea, Xiaoyong Du, Orhun Kara, Ting Liu,
Dominik Ślęzak, and Xiaokang Yang

Editorial Board

More information about this series at http://www.springer.com/series/7899

Miguel Botto-Tobar · Julio Barzola-Monteses
Eduardo Santos-Baquerizo
Mayken Espinoza-Andaluz
Wendy Yánez-Pazmiño (Eds.)

Computer and Communication Engineering

First International Conference, ICCCE 2018
Guayaquil, Ecuador, October 25–27, 2018
Proceedings

Springer

Editors
Miguel Botto-Tobar (iD)
Eindhoven University of Technology
Eindhoven, The Netherlands

Eduardo Santos-Baquerizo
University of Guayaquil
Guayaquil, Ecuador

Wendy Yánez-Pazmiño
University of Birmingham
Birmingham, UK

Julio Barzola-Monteses
University of Guayaquil
Guayaquil, Ecuador

Mayken Espinoza-Andaluz
Escuela Superior Politécnica del Litoral
(ESPOL)
Guayaquil, Ecuador

ISSN 1865-0929 ISSN 1865-0937 (electronic)
Communications in Computer and Information Science
ISBN 978-3-030-12017-7 ISBN 978-3-030-12018-4 (eBook)
https://doi.org/10.1007/978-3-030-12018-4

Library of Congress Control Number: 2018968416

This Springer imprint is published by the registered company Springer Nature Switzerland AG
The registered company address is: Gewerbestrasse 11, 6330 Cham, Switzerland

Preface

The First International Conference on Computer and Communication Engineering (ICCCE 2018), was held on the main campus of the University of Guayaquil (UG), in Guayaquil, Ecuador, during October 25–27, 2018, and it was organized and supported by the Department of Mathematics and Physical Sciences at the University of Guayaquil, Ecuador. The ICCCE series aims to become the most important scientific event for updating, training, innovation, and dissemination in advanced studies and generation of knowledge. It brings together top researchers and practitioners working in different domains in the field of computer science and information systems to exchange their expertise and to discuss the perspectives of development and collaboration in these areas. The content of this volume is related to the following subjects:

- Communications
    - Networking protocols and performance
- Computer and software engineering
    - Software engineering
    - Information systems
    - Computational intelligence

ICCC 2018 received 68 submissions written in English by 133 authors coming from 10 different countries. All these papers were peer-reviewed by the ICCCE 2018 Program Committee consisting of 40 high-quality researchers. To assure a high-quality and thoughtful review process, we assigned each paper at least three reviewers. Based on the peer reviews, 12 full papers were accepted, resulting in an 18% acceptance rate, which was within our goal of less than 40%.

We would like to express our sincere gratitude to the invited speakers for their inspirational talks, to the authors for submitting their works to this conference, and the reviewers for sharing their experience during the selection process.

October 2018

Miguel Botto-Tobar
Julio Barzola-Monteses
Eduardo Santos-Baquerizo
Mayken Espinoza-Andaluz
Wendy Yánez-Pazmiño

Organization

Honorary Committee

Galo Salcedo Rosales	Universidad de Guayaquil, Ecuador
Gulnara Borja Cabrera	Universidad de Guayaquil, Ecuador
Eduardo Santos-Baquerizo	Universidad de Guayaquil, Ecuador/Escuela Superior Politécnica del Litoral (ESPOL), Ecuador
Javier Córdova Rizo	Universidad de Guayaquil, Ecuador

Organizing Committee

Miguel Botto-Tobar	Eindhoven University of Technology, The Netherlands
Julio Barzola-Monteses	Universidad de Guayaquil, Ecuador
Eduardo Santos-Baquerizo	Universidad de Guayaquil, Ecuador/Escuela Superior Politécnica del Litoral (ESPOL), Ecuador
Mayken Espinoza-Andaluz	Escuela Superior Politécnica del Litoral, Ecuador
Wendy Yánez-Pazmiño	University of Birmingham, UK

Local Committee

Eduardo Santos-Baquerizo	Universidad de Guayaquil, Ecuador/Escuela Superior Politécnica del Litoral (ESPOL), Ecuador
Javier Córdova Rizo	Universidad de Guayaquil, Ecuador
Lorenzo Cevallos-Torres	Universidad de Guayaquil, Ecuador
Carlos Mora Cabrera	Universidad de Guayaquil, Ecuador
Abel Alarcón Salvatierra	Universidad de Guayaquil, Ecuador
Harry Luna Aveiga	Universidad de Guayaquil, Ecuador
Christian Antón Cedeño	Universidad de Guayaquil, Ecuador
Luis Alonso Águila	Universidad de Guayaquil, Ecuador
Víctor Padilla Farías	Universidad de Guayaquil, Ecuador
Ruth Paredes Santín	Universidad de Guayaquil, Ecuador

Program Committee

José Medina Moreira	University of Murcia, Spain
Julio Albuja Sánchez	James Cook University, Australia
Julio Barzola-Monteses	Sapienza University of Rome, Italy
Gustavo Andrade Miranda	Polytechnic University of Madrid, Spain
Voltaire Bazurto Blacio	University of Victoria, Canada
Guilherme Avelino	Federal University of Piauí, Brazil

Alfredo Núñez	New York University, USA
Allan Avendaño Sudario	Sapienza University of Rome, Italy
Holger Ortega Martínez	University College London, UK
Gabriel Barros Gavilanes	National Polytechnic Institute of Toulouse, France
Ángel Cuenca-Ortega	Polytechnic University of Valencia, Spain
Carlos Barriga Abril	University of Nottingham, UK
Andres Cueva Costales	University of Melbourne, Australia
Mayken Espinoza-Andaluz	Lund University, Sweden
Felipe Ebert	Federal University of Pernambuco, Brazil
Christian Antón Cedeño	University of Guayaquil, Ecuador
María José Escalante Guevara	University of Michigan, USA
Katty Lagos Ortiz	University of Murcia, Spain
Fernando Flores Pulgar	University of Lyon, France
Manuel Beltrán Prado	University of Queensland, Australia
Pablo León Paliz	Université de Neuchâtel, Switzerland
Wilmer Calle Morales	Saint Petersburg, Russia
Eric Moyano Luna	University of Southampton, UK
Pedro García Arias	University of Granma, Cuba
Andres Carrera Rivera	University of Melbourne, Australia
Yan Pacheco Mafla	Royal Institute of Technology, Sweden
Andrés Chango Macas	Polytechnic University of Madrid, Spain
Eduardo Flores Morán	University of Newcastle, UK
Jorge Charco Aguirre	Polytechnic University of Valencia, Spain
Lucia Rivadeneira Barreiro	Nanyang Technological University, Singapore
Ginger Saltos Bernal	University of Portsmouth, UK
Verónica Mendoza Morán	Polytechnic University of Madrid, Spain
Daniel Magües Martínez	Autonomous University of Madrid, Spain
Karla Abad Sacoto	Autonomous University of Barcelona, Spain
Gissela Uribe Nogales	McGill University, Canada
Carlos Valarezo Loiza	Manchester University, UK
Iván Valarezo Lozano	University of Melbourne, Australia
Alexandra Velasco Arévalo	Universität Stuttgart, Germany
Verónica Yépez Reyes	South Danish University, Denmark
Alejandro Ramos Nolazco	Monterrey Institute of Technology and Advanced Studies, Mexico

Sponsoring Institutions

Universidad de Guayaquil
http://www.ug.edu.ec

http://www.fcmf.ug.edu.ec

Contents

Communications

Platform Model for the Integration of Users with Distributed Energy Resources in Distribution Networks

Luis A. Arias[1]([✉]), Edwin Rivas[2], and Francisco Santamaria[2]

[1] Faculty of Engineering, Universidad Autónoma de Colombia,
Bogotá, Colombia
lincarias@yahoo.com,
laariasb@correo.udistrital.edu.co
[2] Faculty of Engineering, Universidad Distrital Francisco José de Caldas,
Bogotá, Colombia
{edwinrivast, fssantamaria}@udistrital.edu.co

Abstract. This paper shows the design phases of a platform model for the integration of users with distributed energy resources (DER) in a distribution network. DER considered are the demand response (DR) and the distributed generation (DG). The paper shows how, through the integration platform, users can become providers of services and energy for the network. For the administration of the platform, there is an integrating agent that interacts with the users and the network operator. The UML (Unified Modeling Language) methodology was used for design.

Keywords: Demand response program · Distributed generation ·
Distribution network · Energy market · Energy utilities · Integrating strategy ·
Optimization

1 Introduction

Nowadays, energy distribution networks keep changing, and it is common to find in them Distributed Energy Resources (DER) such as Distributed Generation (DG) sources, storage systems and users with Demand Response (DR) programs [1]. Users who are owners of DG and DR resources can supply energy and complementary services to the network operator [2–5].

The integration of DER in distribution networks plays a very important role in their development, with the purpose of guaranteeing normal operating conditions from a technical and economic standpoint. They also contribute to dealing with failures and contingencies of the network as well as performing maintenance [6]. At the economic level, the integration of DER allows the network operator to cut the investments in wiring infrastructure and transformers to meet an ever-expanding demand. Therefore, it is important to analyze possible variability scenarios in the demand, including electric vehicles and energy storage systems in future operation of the network. To achieve this, authors such as [7, 8] state that there are three fundamental pillars for future

© Springer Nature Switzerland AG 2019
M. Botto-Tobar et al. (Eds.): ICCCE 2018, CCIS 959, pp. 3–14, 2019.
https://doi.org/10.1007/978-3-030-12018-4_1

management and integration in networks: demand-side management, electric vehicle charging systems, and intelligent storage systems.

In this article, the design of an access platform for DER integration is shown. The considered resources are the DG and DR elements owned by the network user. By manipulating DER, users become suppliers of two types of energy products for the network operator. The first product is energy at the distribution level and the second product encompasses complementary services for the network operator, such as coverage of demand peaks or improvement of voltage profiles.

The paper is organized as follows. Section 2 describes some forms of DER integration proposed by specialized literature; Sect. 3 describes the IEEE 34-node network used for testing as well as the power delivered by its users. Section 4 describes the methodology which includes a list of the main requirements of the platform and the characteristics of the actors involved in the management of DER through the integration platform. In UML, a use case diagram is built which is an extended form of a use case and a class diagram. The operation details of the platform for selling the disconnection service are described in the form of sequence diagrams. Finally, conclusions and recommendations are given on the potential of the DER integration platform.

2 Integration of DER

Specialized literature has proposed DER integration solutions based on SCADA (Supervisory Control Acquisition Data) systems that are often used in tasks such as network management, data reception from sensing devices that monitor the substations and protection offered by devices that can alter their scope in terms of the connection or disconnection of DG elements. Subsystems knowns as microgrids are another solution that enable the integration of DG resources and the loads associated with DR programs.

In [9], the management of the distribution network that integrates DER is explained. Real-time participation in price market is achieved through the use of microgrids focusing on autonomous energy networks characterized by a high level of DER penetration. Microgrids constitute a very interesting strategy, particularly for integral energy solutions which would include not only electricity supply, but also gas and heating [10].

Some authors present a management model for the Integration of DER, supported by Virtual Power Plants (VPP), seen as service-oriented software architectures [11]. Three scenarios are discussed: 1. An initial scenario places the VPP as the central axis to where the DER converges, comprising DG elements, storage devices and controllers for point loads. 2. An intermediate scenario includes several auxiliary VPP that manage the DER of each microgrid, which in turn are controlled by a central VPP. 3. A third scenario contemplates a centralized service system offering VPP services and managing the information received from the network's environment. Such information involves the status of the trunks adjacent to each microgrid as well as the meteorological status and its forecasts for DG sources and real-time energy prices. VPP facilitate the integration of DER, allowing to overcome to a large extent inconveniences related to the uncertain behavior of DER such as DG elements, thanks to the parallel management of storage system associated technologies and DR mechanisms [12].

In Table 1, a comparative summary of the SCADA, Microgrid and VPP systems is shown, seeing them as DER integration strategies.

Table 1. Comparative summary of DER integration strategies

Factor	SCADA	Microgrid	Virtual Power Plant
Main objective	Control of DG devices, occasionally DR	Control/Integration of DER in the network	Management/Control and Integration of DER
Application range	Network elements	Local sectors of the network	Without any restrictions
Infrastructure	Control elements, sensors	AMI (Advanced Measurements Instruments) devices, flow measurers, communications technology	AMI devices, flow measurers, communications technology and energy market links
Operation	Centralized	With the network or through islanding	Centralized or decentralized
Focus	Technical efficiency of network elements	Energy efficiency of the microgrid	Energy and economic efficiency of the network
Functional elements	Control of DG, management of DR mechanisms	DG control, storage control and DR	Coordination/Control of DG, DR, storage systems, compensating elements, integration of electric vehicles

3 IEEE 34-Node Network

The proposed design of the platform is oriented towards the management of connected users within an IEEE network of 34 nodes. However, it can be extended to more complex networks. The 34-node IEEE model considers the powers associated with each load shown in Table 2.

The underlined loads are those that participate in the DR program. The selection process of the loads is determined by the largest amounts of installed power. Figure 1 shows the topology of the radial type distribution network used as in the testing scenario. For the users' power levels, the recommended values for a standard IEEE 34-node network were taken as reference from [13, 14].

Table 3 shows the manageable power of the users participating in the DR program. It also shows the type of DG source of some users and their power. This data enables the characterization of the users that will enter the integration platform.

Table 2. Power parameters for IEEE 34-node network loads

Load	Power		Load	Power	
	Active (kW)	Reactive (kVAr)		Active (kW)	Reactive (kVAr)
816	5	2,5	824	24,5	12
842	5	2,5	806	27,5	14,5
864	5	2,5	802	27,5	14,5
856	5	2,5	846	34	17
854	5	2,5	**840**	**47**	**31**
828	5,5	2,5	**830**	**48,5**	**21,5**
832	7,5	3,5	**836**	**61**	**31,5**
810	8	4	**822**	**67,5**	**35**
808	8	4	**848**	**71,5**	**53,5**
862	14	7	**820**	**84,5**	**43,5**
838	14	7	**834**	**89**	**45**
818	17	8,5	**860**	**174**	**106**
826	20	10	**844**	**432**	**329**
858	24,5	12,5	**890**	**450**	**225**

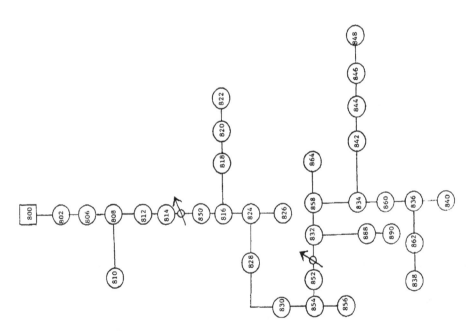

Fig. 1. IEEE 34-node network model used for testing

Table 3. Characteristic parameters of the users for the test scenario.

User	Total power, kVA	Manageable power, kW	DG	P_{DG}, kVA
840	47	3.2	-	
830	48.5	3.395	-	
836	61	4.27	-	
822	67.5	4.725	-	
848	71.5	5.005	-	
820	84.5	5.915	-	
834	89	6.23	Photovoltaic	10
860	174	12.18	Photovoltaic	15
844	432	30.24	-	
890	450	31.5	Microturbine	125

4 Methodology

The DER integration platform was designed by following these phases: *Definition of the approach*, then *Analysis and list of requirements*. Subsequently, the main use cases and the extended use cases were established. This was followed by the *Verification of compliance* of extended use cases with the list of requirements. When the requirements are not satisfied, the use case diagrams are adjusted accordingly. If the result of the verification phase is positive, then the sequence diagrams are created showing the exchange messages of the DER integration platform each time that an energy service is required such as a request of power disconnection. Lastly, the corresponding class diagrams are made while specifying variables such as the manageable power and DG power manipulated by the actors of the platform as well as the methods involved in their work.

Figure 2 shows the flow diagram of the design phases of the DER integration platform.

4.1 Definition and Analysis of Requirements

The requirements describe in a narrative way the elements, tasks and characteristics that make up the DER integration platform. For their individualization, the main considerations of the initial approach stage are adopted, by assigning a priority level to each one according to their importance within the platform. The total number of requirements used to analyze the characteristics of the platform surpassed 100. Table 4 shows some of the main requirements that characterize the functionality of the integration platform.

As seen in Table 4, the requirement R013 describes how users can choose at which times of the day they are available to participate in DR-based services and distributed generation resources. Requirement R082 indicates that the network operator must have a section in the platform for the generation of service demands to the integrating agent.

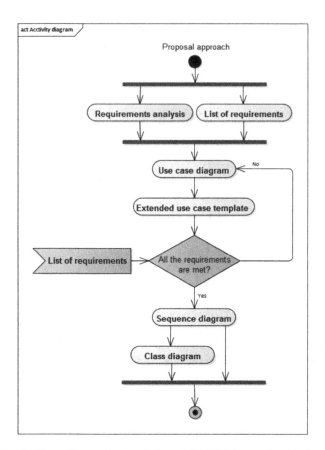

Fig. 2. Flow diagram for the design of the DER integration platform

4.2 Use Cases Diagrams

After establishing the list of requirements and their respective analysis, the use case diagram is created. It shows the actors of the DER integration system: the integrating agent, the network operator and the users (Fig. 3).

The use case diagram shows that the integrating agent performs three management tasks on the platform: user management, interaction with the network operator and management/control of the DER. Each task of the integrating agent is interpreted as an additional use case as follows: User management includes the registration of users on the platform and their permanent communication with the integrating agent. During the registration process, users state their identification data, power level and the DR or DG resources that they own. As an example, Table 5 exhibits the extended data of one user referenced in Table 2.

As it can be noticed, the users participating in the DR program can specify their ID, their installed power as well as their manageable power, i.e., the power that they can disconnect at any given moment. Furthermore, the user can indicate the type and power of his DG source as well as the hours of the day in which he can disconnect the

Table 4. List of requirements

ID	Description	Priority
R013	The software must have an application that provides comfort to the user in the management of scheduled disconnections	High
R018	The software must store and manage distributed generation information and pertinent user data	High
R020	Within the software, the user must have the option to cancel a scheduled disconnection that takes place within a pre-established time	High
R029	The website must store personal and technical data from each user in an encrypted way inside a database	High
R064	The site must be designed to interact with different software and generate graphics and data corresponding to the requested information	High
R076	The software should provide simulated results of the network state based on certain disconnections	High
R079	The software must determine the most efficient way to assign a technician to the users	High
R082	The software must allow the network operator to make power disconnection or reduction requests	High
R090	The site must be designed to control and manage petitions of emergency power disconnection requested by the network operator as a priority order	High
R104	The webpage must enable the technician to input the technical data of a user	High

manageable power, the variable costs (CV_{ih}) and the fixed cost (CF_i). The latter is associated to the maintenance of the communications and the control of the infrastructure that the integrating agent uses to switch between manageable power loads.

With regard to the interaction with the network operator, the integrating agent can receive orders or demands from him. The network operator may request that the energy consumption is reduced throughout the day or that the consumption peaks are cut at certain times of the day. In such cases, the integration platform receives information from the operator in the form described in Table 6.

The data in Table 6 can be interpreted as the disconnection demand vector D_h representing the power quantities that need to be reduced for each hour. There are some hours that do not require any power reduction (marked by a hyphen "-").

The interactions between the integrating agent and the network operator include activities related to the economic and technical evaluation, thereby solving optimization problems. The solution of the economic optimization problem allows to adjust the offer of the integrating agent.

The target function is shown in Eq. 1

$$min \sum_{h}^{24} \sum_{i}^{N} [CF_i * Z_{ih} + CV_{ih} * P_{ih}] \qquad (1)$$

Z_{ih} is a parameter equal to 1 if the user participates in the DR program and equal to 0 in the opposite scenario.

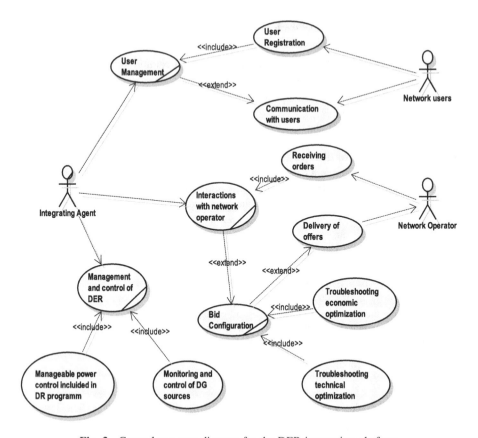

Fig. 3. General use case diagram for the DER integration platform

Table 5. Extended data of *User 834* registration in the platform

User ID	834			
Installed power, kW	Manageable power, kW	Type of DG		P_{DG}, kVA
89	6,23	Photovoltaic		10

Participation schedule in the DR program, hours																							
1	2	3	4	5	6	7	8	9	10	11	12	13	14	15	16	17	18	19	20	21	22	23	24
0	0	1	0	0	0	1	1	0	0	0	0	0	0	0	0	0	1	1	0	0	0	0	0

CV_{th}	0.02 USD/kWh	0.03 USD/kWh	0.022 USD/kWh
CF_i	0.025 USD/kWh		

Table 6. Power disconnection requirements during some hours of the day, D_h

Id No.	0001																							
Hour	1	2	3	4	5	6	7	8	9	10	11	12	13	14	15	16	17	18	19	20	21	22	23	24
kW	20	10	30	-	-	-	30	35	30	-	-	-	-	-	-	-	20	20	25	35	10	-	-	-

P_{ih} is the power disconnected by a user at a certain time of the day.

s.to.

$$\sum_{i=1}^{N} P_{ih} \geq D_h \tag{2}$$

where $h = 1, 2, 3, \ldots, 24$ represent the hours of the day

$$0 \leq P_{ih} \leq P_i * Z_{ih} \tag{3}$$

P_i is the total manageable power of each user

$$\sum_{h=1}^{24} Z_{ih} \leq KMAX_i \tag{4}$$

$KMAX_i$ is the maximum number of participation times for each user.

Restrictions:
The first restriction is related to the coverage of the demand made in each hour (Eq. 2). The second restriction refers to the limits of the maximum unplugged power for each user when it is requested to participate in the DR program (Eq. 3). The third restriction involves the maximum number of times that a user can participate in the DR program throughout the day (Eq. 4). Every user is conditioned to participate for a limited number of times per day.

The final activity of the integrating agent's use case is the coordination of DER. On one hand, the integrating agent can effectively connect or disconnect the user's manageable loads. On the other hand, he monitors and controls the DG sources which can be either deterministic (such as the case of User 890 that has a 125 kVA microturbine) or stochastic (such as the case of User 830 that has a photovoltaic source of 10 kVA). If the source is deterministic, the integrating agent monitors its power level and operating status. For stochastic sources, the integrating agent evaluates the current power levels and monitors the behavior of the resource through probability density functions.

In the management activity of the DG sources, an energy dispatch offer is established for them, considering their behavior. This offer is sent to the network operator, which then has two options: 1. To buy said energy if the offered quantity lies in the surplus energy category or 2. To request that the integrating agent solves an optimization problem that allows the operator to reach the minimum cost per kWh. In its general form, the optimization problem of energy dispatch is shown below (Eqs. 5 and 6).

$$\text{Min} \, FO_{GD1} + FO_{GD2} + \ldots + FO_{GDn} \tag{5}$$

FO_{GDn} is the target function for each DG source

s.to.

$$P_{GD1} + P_{GD2} + \ldots + P_{GDn} \geq D_{NO} \tag{6}$$

D_{NO} is the energy demand request by the network operator.

4.3 Sequence Diagram

In sequence diagrams, the interaction between the components of the system over time is shown for the previously explained use cases. As an example, Fig. 4 details the sequence diagram for the sale of a disconnection service to the network operator.

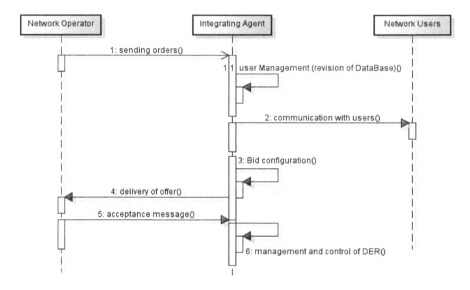

Fig. 4. Sequence diagram for selling a disconnection service of manageable power

The network operator sends a power disconnection request for several hours. The integrating agent receives the order and checks the user database. Then, he sends a message to confirm the participation of the users. The users respond and thus the integrating agent can set an offer and send it to the network operator.

To establish the offer, the integrative agent must solve an optimization problem such as the one specified in Eqs. 1 to 6 where the available DER are used while seeking the lowest cost for each hour according to network operator's demands. When the operator accepts, the integrating agent sends control messages to the users' manageable loads.

4.4 Class Diagram

Figure 5 shows the class diagram of the main actors in the DER integration platform: the integrative agent, the network operator and the users.

The class diagram shows the identification data of the integrative agent, the network operator and the users (ID). The integrative agent manages the users which implies being in charge of registering users, sending confirmation messages, connecting and disconnecting manageable loads and DG elements. Additionally, the agent interacts with the network operator by receiving requests for both energy and disconnection services and responds to such requests using the users' DER.

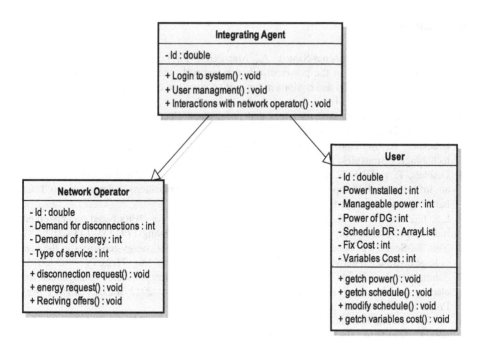

Fig. 5. Class diagram for the main actors in the integration platform

The network operator class shows variables such as the disconnection request and energy demand vector. The operator sends the requests to the integrating agent and then receives the offers sent to him. Operator decides whether he accepts them or not depending on the resulting cost. The user class diagram delivers variables such as the manageable power, DG power and the disconnection timetable for said manageable power. Integrating agent also states the fixed and variables costs of the disconnected kW and the energy offered. Some of his methods include the modification of the disconnection timetables to which he commits to and the modification of the variable costs per disconnected kW for each hour of the day.

5 Conclusions

The designed model of the integration platform is versatile and works for an unlimited number of users. It gathers the management-related characteristics of the distributed energy resources that are currently requested to the distribution networks. Modeling with UML allows the platform to be open to any type of software, hardware technology or search engine found on the Internet.

The inclusion of the capacity to solve optimization problems in the integration platform makes it an effective tool for managing the resources of the network, thereby diminishing the impact of a massive participation of DER.

References

1. Ruiz-Romero, S., Colmenar-Santos, A., Mur-Pérez, F., López-Rey, Á.: Integration of distributed generation in the power distribution network: the need for smart grid control systems, communication and equipment for a smart city - use cases. Renew. Sustain. Energy Rev. **38**, 223–234 (2014)
2. Ackermann, T.: Distributed resources and re-regulated electricity markets. Electr. Power Syst. Res. **77**(9), 1148–1159 (2007)
3. Bruckner, T., Morrison, R., Wittmann, T.: Public policy modeling of distributed energy technologies: strategies, attributes, and challenges. Ecol. Econ. **54**(2–3), 328–345 (2005)
4. Dethlefs, T., Preisler, T., Renz, W., Hamburg, H.A.W., Tor, B.: A DER Registry System as an Infrastructural Component for future Smart Grid Applications Approaches on Data handling and main, pp. 93–99 (2015)
5. Lai, J., Zhou, H., Lu, X., Liu, Z.: Distributed power control for DERs based on networked multiagent systems with communication delays. Neurocomputing **179**, 135–143 (2016)
6. You, S., Segerberg, H.: Integration of 100% micro-distributed energy resources in the low voltage distribution network: a Danish case study. Appl. Therm. Eng. **71**(2), 797–808 (2013)
7. Schmutzler, J., Wietfeld, C., Andersen, C.A.: Distributed energy resource management for electric vehicles using IEC 61850 and ISO/IEC 15118. In: 2012 IEEE Vehicle Power Propulsion Conference, pp. 1457–1462 (2012)
8. Muñoz-Álvarez, D., Cadena, Á.I., Alzate, J.M.: Integrating variable distributed generation within short-term electricity markets. In: 2012 IEEE PES Innovative Smart Grid Technologies, ISGT 2012, pp. 1–8 (2012)
9. Dobakhshari, A.S., Azizi, S., Ranjbar, A.M.: Control of microgrids: aspects and prospects. In: 2011 International Conference on Networking, Sensing and Control, ICNSC 2011, pp. 38–43, April 2011
10. Ramírez, A., Chica, A.: MicroRed inteligente sustentable de biogás para zona no interconectada (2013)
11. Andersen, P.B., Poulsen, B., Decker, M., Traeholt, C., Ostergaard, J.: Evaluation of a Generic Virtual Power Plant framework using service oriented architecture. In: 2008 IEEE 2nd International Power Energy Conference, pp. 1212–1217 (2008)
12. Dietrich, K., Latorre, J.M., Olmos, L., Ramos, A.: Modelling and assessing the impacts of self supply and market-revenue driven Virtual Power Plants. Electr. Power Syst. Res. **119**, 462–470 (2015)
13. Fu, Q., et al.: Generation capacity design for a microgrid for measurable power quality indexes. In: 2012 IEEE PES Innovative Smart Grid Technologies, ISGT 2012, pp. 1–6 (2012)
14. Balamurugan, K., Srinivasan, D., Reindl, T.: Impact of distributed generation on power distribution systems. Energy Proc. **25**, 93–100 (2012)

Evaluation of Digital Terrestrial Television as a Tool for Supporting Dyslexia Therapies

Eduardo Antonio Alvarado Unamuno$^{(\boxtimes)}$ ⓘ,
Christian Roberto Antón Cedeño ⓘ,
Jenny Elizabeth Arízaga Gamboa ⓘ, and Jorge Chicala Arroyave ⓘ

Universidad de Guayaquil, Cdla. Universitaria Salvador Allende,
Guayaquil, Ecuador
{eduardo.alvaradou, christian.antonc, jenny.arizagag,
jorge.chicalaa}@ug.edu.ec

Abstract. The sole purpose of this study is to evaluate the outcome of the feasibility involved with the ergonomic and key point of view that incorporate the Digital Terrestrial Television (DTT) technologies as an add-on tool supporting therapies for children with Developmental or Evolutionary Dyslexia, taking this as a case study for children of TecnoMedic Rehabilitation Center of Medical Technology School of Universidad de Guayaquil. The DTT application was developed based on basic therapy composed of four levels of complexity on which were proposed by the speech therapists of the Medical Technology School of Universidad de Guayaquil. Three variables were determined for their analysis with respect to the reeducation of the perceptive-motor, language and reading. The data was obtained before, during and after the use of the software for which a satisfactory of compliance survey was also carried out for children and speech therapists. Considering that Ecuador adhered to the Brazilian DTT standard, the technological tools used were those proposed by the creators of such standard.

Keywords: Digital Terrestrial Television · Developmental Dyslexia · Ginga · Set-top Box

1 Introduction

Television is a venue of mass dissemination with a high scale of consumption, so Ecuador, until 2012, had 9 out of 10 households with color television; Ecuadorians watch television around 3 h a day on average [1], Digital Terrestrial Television also known by its abbreviation "TDT" is a new way of transmitting free or open television signals with advantages such as higher quality video, image and sound. With the transmission in digital format, it will be possible to take advantage of the radio spectrum and frequency bands will be released for the use of new technologies. To adopt Digital Terrestrial Television, there are four standards in force worldwide, and each country uses the one that best suits its needs. Ecuador, chose the ISDB-T International standard on March 25, 2010 [1].

© Springer Nature Switzerland AG 2019
M. Botto-Tobar et al. (Eds.): ICCCE 2018, CCIS 959, pp. 15–30, 2019.
https://doi.org/10.1007/978-3-030-12018-4_2

In contrast to analogue television that encodes images and sounds in an analogous way, digital television encodes images and sounds in a digital way, allowing better image quality, access to multiple channels and interactive services, which is why digital television provides the opportunity to create interactive applications, hence the name Interactive Digital Television (TVDI). With TVDI, the consumer can go from being a passive viewer and become an active participant. Television goes from being merely a diffuser of content to enabling access to content. Through TVDI, it may be possible to access a set of public or private services that cover various fields such as commerce, administrative management, entertainment and learning. You can list services such as shopping, tele banking, telemedicine, games, email, a variety of information services (pharmacies on duty, alerts, weather, news, sports, traffic, etc.) [2].

Interactivity refers to the versatility of a program so that user decisions can change their course. It represents the control that the person can exercise over the program and the malleability that it presents to accommodate the decisions of the person who uses it [3].

Interactivity allows a dialogue where the participant has the capacity to intervene in programs or services that he/she receives. There are two types of local or remote interactivity. On the first case, the consumer accesses interactive content without sending data to the issuer, and on the second case, there is a return channel through which to send data and interact with both the service provider and other consumers.

Dyslexia-According to the American Psychiatric Association, through the DSM-V (Diagnostic and Statistical Manual of Mental Disorders, 2013) indicates: "Dyslexia is an alternative term used to refer to a pattern of learning difficulties that is characterized for problems with the recognition of words in a precise or fluid way, misspelling and poor spelling ability" [4], given that previous works were found in which through video games, the reading of children with Dyslexia was improved [5] and the use of computer programs in speech therapies indicates the advantage of such programs in these treatments [6], in present work, digital television is used to develop local interactive services as an audio visual support tool for intervention of developmental dyslexia.

1.1   Related Work

There are previous tasks where the interactivity of DTT is used as EsCoTDT (Platform of Cognitive Stimulation through TDT-MHP) [7] which helps to strengthen the maintenance of cognitive abilities in Parkinson patients. Through this platform, patients with Parkinson can perform cognitive stimulation therapy from their own home using interactive digital television, thus complementing therapies taught in the Association of Parkinson of Madrid.

iFunnyCube is an interactive DTT application which is used in rehabilitation of people with special needs. In Brazil, they have applied it to a group of people with Down syndrome. The application is a game with cubes that allows the classification of ways that help in process of cognitive development and motor coordination of the child [8].

ImFine is an application in which interactive DTT is used to track older adults where not only the doctor, but also the friends perform this follow-up work. It is similar to Twitter but with a different approach when using. In ImFine, a person has several protectors that track their actions [8].

2 Dyslexia

There are several definitions that have been given to this term. Two different statements coined by organizations specialized in this difficulty are presented.

According to the definition adopted by the World Federation of Neurology in 1968 [9] dyslexia is a problem that is characterized by a deficit in learning to read despite receiving correct teaching, showing normal intelligence and enjoying normal socio-cultural opportunities.

For its part, the International Dyslexia Association defines it as a specific learning disability of neurobiological origin, characterized by difficulties with precise and/or fluid word recognition and poor spelling and decoding. These difficulties are often the result of a deficit in the phonological component of language that is often unexpected in relation to other cognitive skills and the provision of effective classroom education. Secondary consequences can include problems in reading comprehension and a reduced reading experience that can impede the growth of vocabulary and prior knowledge [10].

From previous definitions [4], it can be inferred that dyslexia is presented as a difficulty in reading learning that is characterized by having problems in the recognition of words, which causes reading and writing incorrectly, being the affected a person with an IQ within the normal average and with a schooling appropriate to his age.

2.1 Types of Dyslexia

Within this theme, we mainly distinguish between acquired dyslexia and developmental dyslexia. Acquired Dyslexia occurs when the person has had some kind of deterioration or brain trauma due to genetic origin, heart attacks or cranial injuries. Within acquired dyslexia there are 2 subtypes: peripheral dyslexia and deep dyslexia [11].

Developmental dyslexia (DD) is the difficulty of learning to read as well as writing, spelling, reading comprehension, etc. This disorder occurs without the individual having any motor, sensory, physical, psychic or intellectual delay, manifesting when they begin to develop reading skills [11]. In general, dyslexic persons are characterized by substituting, omitting or inverting graphemes and not recognizing phonemes corresponding to them.

DD usually presents characteristics associated with age ranges of individuals comprised in: (1) 3 to 5 years, (2) 6 to 11 years and (3) 12 years or more. Given that the present study was carried out in children between the ages of 9 and 11 who are in the second range, these usually present the characteristics shown in Table 1 and that allow identifying this type of disorder for treatment.

2.2 Intervention of Children with Developmental Dyslexia

The intervention of people with developmental dyslexia is performed after a complete and individualized diagnosis. The approach to this disorder must be multidisciplinary, involving psychologists, speech therapists, educational psychologists, teachers and parents. There are 3 levels in which reeducation can be planned, the first is the level of prevention or initiation, which is based on preventing the learning difficulties of

Table 1. Characteristics of children with DD according to age range.

Children from 6 to 11 years old
They usually invert words numbers and letters
Confusion in words with the order of their letters
Problems to relate the sound with the letter
They have difficulty in pronunciation of words
They replace or invert syllables
They usually confuse the writing of left and right, mirror writing
Poor motor coordination, difficulty saying and giving thoughts
Bad calligraphy
They usually have difficulty following verbal instructions and completing series
Poor reading comprehension
Grammar and deficit spelling misuse of grammar and spelling
Inability to apply calculations or problem solving with simple numerical concepts

reading and writing in children of initial age, the second level is reeducation, here it is about correcting to a great extent the acquired learning difficulties, it is advisable to apply it in children not older than 10 years and the last one is the level of consolidation, based on stabilizing the acquired knowledge and intervening any dyslexic difficulty that may arise in the child [12].

According to the intervention model suggested by the speech therapist, psychologists, and psycho-pedagogues, various strategies will be applied [13], among them we mention, the daily work with rhymes, identify phrases and words, train patients in oral motor perception, nowadays Computational cognitive training is also used [13] in which computer applications are used as a complement to classic exercises.

In this work, an application was developed as a complement in the level of reeducation where the following areas are covered: Perceptive-Motive, Language and Reading.

In the Perceptive-Motor area, you can work on the body outline, laterality, spatial orientation and words, making visual discriminations of them. As for reading, the therapist will color a text so that it is analyzed correctly by mean of questions.

3 Digital Terrestrial Television (DTT)

Digital Terrestrial Television (DTT) or Open Digital Television (TDA) is an evolution of analog television where the transmission and reception of images and sounds are made by digital signals in the same band of analog broadcast, but being binary takes advantage of the radio spectrum providing the ability to broadcast more channels in the same space that currently occupies a single analog channel, also higher image and sound quality; in addition, it allows extra services that boost up value to the programming. The emission of the signal is done by a transmitting antenna or terrestrial repeaters up to a UHF antenna connected to a set-top box (STB) or a television with the standard applied in the country.

Several standards have been developed for digital television and each country has taken the one that best suits its technical and political needs. The standards for digital television are: ATSC, DVB-T which has a second generation that is DVB-T2, ISDBT, ISDBTb or SBTVD and DTMB [14], in Ecuador the ISDBTb standard was adopted, which is a variant Brazilian of the ISDBT standard of Japan, the main difference is that the video coding for the Japanese standard is H.264 and for the Brazilian it is MPEG-2.

A complete digital television (DTV) system consists of three parts: the head-end transmitter system, the transmission system/distribution network and the user terminal system. Our major analysis will focus on the last one describing its architecture and its ability to interact locally.

3.1   Set-Top Box

In digital television to watch a program, you can use a digital TV that already includes the tuner for DTV or an STB connected to an analog TV, the STBs are often used for their low cost, they are constituted by a layer of hardware and software. In Fig. 1, the typical internal structure of STB has four layers: hardware, device driver, middleware, and a layer of software applications; additionally, there is a conditioned access module (CA) that is an encryption mechanism for the content of the programs according to the user groups and service modes [14].

The remote control is an electronic device used to control a remote device. Interactive digital television becomes a tool to access the menus of applications. There are studies on the ease of using DTT remote controls [15], where the objective was to find an intuitive and easy-to-use remote control based on the labeling of the buttons, comparative studies of remote controls for digital television have also been carried out in the United Kingdom [16], where it is determined which is the proper distribution and labeling of the remote control buttons to improve the user experience of DTT in the country [17]. In this study, the red, blue, yellow and green buttons of the remote control will be used to access the interactive screens.

3.2   GINGA Middleware

In programming environments for DTV, support is provided for the execution of interactive applications in two environments: a declarative and an imperative. In the Brazilian digital TV system, the declarative environment is represented by Ginga-NCL, which supports applications based on the NCL (Nested Context Language) and the imperative environment is represented by Ginga-J, which provides support for the execution of applications written in Java language. Ginga is the middleware that will allow communication between the application and the execution infrastructure destined for the SBTVD, a standard established by Brazil that is a modification of the Japanese standard.

According to the recommendation, ITU H.761E is not only optimal for digital television but also for television by internet protocol (IPTV) [19]. The institutions involved in the creation of this technology are Telemídia Lab together with LAViD and LIFIA [20]. Brazil has contemplated several standards for the standard published by the SBTVD Forum [21].

Ginga Architecture

The Ginga architecture is observed in Fig. 1 and can be divided into three main modules: Ginga Common Core (Ginga-CC), Ginga-NCL and Ginga-J, the last two modules form the specific services of Ginga [22].

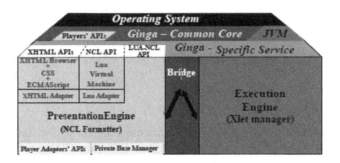

Fig. 1. Ginga Architecture [22].

Common Core

The Common Core allows communication between the operating system and the hardware, as well as the link between declarative and imperative languages through its components. It is in charge of tuning channels through the tuner; after that, the selection filters allow to pass information required by the APIs through the data processor, the Common Core accesses, processes and transports information.

Ginga NCL is the module responsible for execution of declarative applications encoded with NCL or hybrid (NCL and LUA). Its infrastructure is made up of the formatter, the design administrator, the converter, the programmer, the private database administrator, the analyzer of XML, the replay manager and the NCL context manager. The formatter captures and controls the applications programmed with the NCL language. The design administrator recognizes the regions established in the application. The programmer evaluates and organizes the links and programming, uses the Player Manager to correctly start the medium content at the right time. The XML parser and the converter work together to translate the NCL language appropriately and then send it to the formatter [23].

NCL

NCL or Nested Context Language is an XML application language that is based on the conceptual data model NCM or Nested Context Model, it allows to incorporate and synchronize multimedia elements such as images, text, sound, videos, etc. This defines the time and place where they will be executed when developing interactive applications [24]. In NCL we work with media elements such as these images, videos, sound and text. To develop in NCL, four questions must be answered: Where will the elements be displayed? What elements will be displayed? How will they be displayed? And when will they be shown?

LUA

LUA is free software that is used as a language for program development and that offers good support for objective-oriented programming, functional programming and data-oriented programming. This language is designed with an extensible and modifiable semantics with the use of metatables, it is imperative, that it sends to the computer a set of instructions on how to perform a task [25]. This progression language is influenced by Scheme, SNOBOL, Modula, CLU, C++ and runs in a virtual machine.

4   Methodology

4.1   Application Design

The design of solution models a basic therapy aimed at patients with Developmental or Evolutionary Dyslexia registered in Medical Therapy Center of Medical Sciences Faculty of Universidad de Guayaquil, this therapy was proposed and supervised by speech therapists from the Medical Technology School of Universidad de Guayaquil. A progressive difficulty index comprised of 4 levels was determined, the first being the most basic with spatial placement exercises, the second level related to word recognition, the third level aimed at meaningfully completing the sentences and the fourth level to interpreting and identify the meaning or idea of a paragraph, this level being the most complex. At the end of each level, the patient obtains his opinion on the use of the remote control as can be seen in Fig. 2 following the same playful scheme proposed by the application.

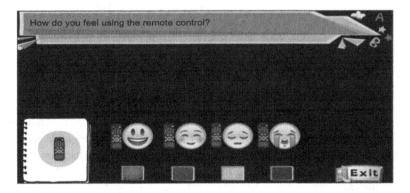

Fig. 2.   Interface to measure the patient's experience in use of remote control.

In order to encourage the participation of the patient, a score scale is determined based on their progress in the levels, this score is presented to the patient at the end of each level and serves as an additional parameter to the work of the speech therapist who evaluates the results independently in each level and in all the exercises included in such a way that the score per action (A) performed is $A = \frac{100/4}{n}$ where (n) represents the number of exercises proposed at a specific level. The final score will be obtained from $\sum_{i=1}^{4}$ nA where (i) represent the level or levels of the application. A management module oriented to the work of the speech therapist was determined for the registration of the orders, images and responses that make up each screen or graphical user or patient interface.

The tools used for the development of applications for DTT are those proposed by the Pontifical Catholic University of Rio (PUC-Río) de Janeiro in Brazil and are available on the website of Telemidia laboratories of PUC-Rio. Figure 3 shows the architecture of the application with the use of blocks created in the LUA language and the Backbone of the application written in NCL, making use of flat files for the persistence of the data that each interface constructs.

Applications Management	LETRITAS Tv	
		Results
		Instructions
	Level 4	Multimedia
		Results
		Instructions
	Level 3	Multimedia
		Results
		Instructions
	Level 2	Multimedia
		Results
		Instructions
	Level 1	Multimedia
	Main	
	Default CommBase	
	Multimedia	

Fig. 3. Architecture of DTT application.

For content management of each graphical interface, an administration module was developed by means of Joomla tool through which the speech therapist builds the therapy by adding the commands and images to each button color in each of the screens, the indicator of the correct answers is also added. The core or backbone of the application consists of two files written in NCL, the first called LetritasTV allows you to manage the flow of information or the program throughout the execution, while the second file named DefaultCommBase manages the distribution of the elements in the regions of the television screen. The graphic scheme of the application provided by the NCL Composer tool shown in Fig. 4 allows to observe the integration of the modules written in LUA, the multimedia and as a basis the NCL.

The components developed in LUA are those that mostly contribute what is known as the business logic to the application because in these modules the work is managed with the multimedia files that are used throughout the execution of the program. For developers, working with LUA is more familiar because it is a programming language with classic control structures, which makes it possible to direct the correct flow of information in an application, whereas NCL is an HTML and HTML style tag language.

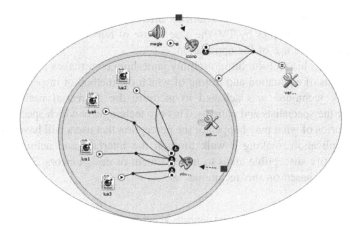

Fig. 4. Visual scheme of application seen in NCL Composer.

XML, in such a way that from a programming point of view, is more flexible than LUA. That is why the PUC-Rio advises the use of the two languages for the development of DTT applications.

The DTT application was evaluated in 20 individuals between 9 and 11 years of age in 2-month trajectory. We attended 4 students per week using a 42″ TV and an STB developer decoder, and with the help of a Flash Drive unit, the software was put in. The therapy was monitored by the speech therapist, only one student per day would be served.

In Level 1 of the application, exercises are proposed for the psychomotor area where it is tried to reaffirm the knowledge of laterality, body schema, spatial notions and temporal notions. Being the therapist who performs the exercises should be coupled to the model of the interface raised in the design.

In Level 2, the therapist performs exercises with letters and syllables, showing their shape, visually discriminating their shape, positioning, relating them to an image, etc. In Level 3, the therapist performs exercises with words, as well as relating them to images, recognition of homonymous and antonym synonymless words, etc. In Level 4, the therapist performs reading comprehension exercises with texts.

The instructions, selected images, options and answers are stored in flat files from administration module. The draw function shows data read on the screen. The correct answer selection for each instruction must be selected by red, blue, yellow or green button on remote control. There are technical considerations for images used in this work, the image format is PNG without any background, so that these are better visualized on the screen, its maximum size is up to 6 MB, although the optimum would be to incorporate images of better quality and small size.

Design of Data Collection Instruments

The Therapy Center of Universidad de Guayaquil, at the time of the investigation, has 20 patients, of which 11 are boys and 9 are girls whose ages fluctuate between 9 and 11 years. Being a small population, sampling techniques will not be applied.

It was determined to create 3 instruments oriented to: Identify the degree of satisfaction of medical therapies by TV, the ease of use of remote control and assess the user experience in the use of the application.

James Hom on his website http://usability.jameshom.com makes a compilation of multiple methods of evaluation and testing of which the method of inspection with the cognitive walk technique was selected to measure the degree of usability of the application by the specialists and patients. This is a technique in which specialists build different scenarios of what may happen or the perception that users will have during the use of the application, making a walk through the interface and acting as a user. Helping to identify susceptible areas to improvement or design errors. Table 2 shows the survey format based on this technique.

Table 2. Survey of therapists and students about the use of the DTT application

Task	Action	Reaction
Access to application	Press red button of remote control	Easy Hard
Access level screen	After pressing red button	Easy Hard
Select a level	Press red, green, yellow or blue button	Easy Hard
Access to interface of selected level	After pressing the control color buttons	Easy Hard
Execution of proposed exercise	Reading the instruction, observing the main image, choosing the correct answer	Easy Hard

5   Results

5.1   Appreciation Level of Tool Acceptance

As part of the field research carried out to study the implementation of the tool, surveys were carried out, at different times of the treatment, on a population of 20 children of both sexes (11 boys and 9 girls) with dyslexia disorder and 5 treating doctors, in order to obtain their point of view regarding the preference to use television as a means to perform the therapy.

Question 1. Would you like to perform the therapies through television (Table 3)?

Table 3. Survey results of predilection for Medical Therapies on TV

	Quantity of boys	Quantity of girls	% Boys	% Girls
YES	10	7	91%	78%
NO	1	2	9%	22%

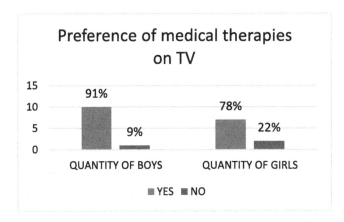

Fig. 5. Preference in use of TV as a means to perform medical therapies

In Fig. 5 we can see a marked taste for use of television as a mean to perform medical therapies related to dyslexia, 91% of boys and 78% of girls have favorably accepted TV as a support to therapies, this tendency can be based on the fact that television is the most used mass media in homes and in front of it children spend the most of their leisure time.

Question 2. How do you feel using remote control (Table 4)?

Table 4. Satisfaction survey results by use of remote control.

	Level 1		Level 2		Level 3		Level 4	
	Boys	Girls	Boys	Girls	Boys	Girls	Boys	Girls
Very happy	4	4	5	5	7	6	9	8
Happy	4	4	4	4	4	3	2	1
Sad	3	1	2	0	0	0	0	0
Very sad	0	0	0	0	0	0	0	0

Figure 6 shows the degree of adaptability that patients have to use remote control for the development of different levels in which therapy has been divided, this tool becomes more familiar to patients as they pass between different levels, in Level 1 only 4 boys and 4 girls felt comfortable with the use of remote control as an interface for their therapy, at the end of Level 4 the satisfaction of using remote control was increased, 9 boys and 8 girls felt comfortable with the use of this device, this is based on consistency of navigation and interaction with the use of colored buttons on remote control.

Question 3. Does the use of application seem easy or difficult (Table 5)?

Both, patients and therapists expressed their complacency in human-machine interaction obtained from the playful design of the DTT application, in Fig. 7 the evaluation made by speech therapists and patients is observed for each of the main

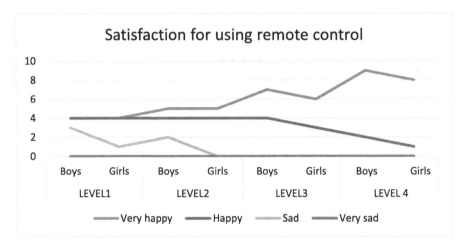

Fig. 6. Satisfaction of use of remote control in levels of medical therapies.

Table 5. Evaluation survey result about user experience in use of application.

	Easy		Hard	
	Therapist	Patient	Therapist	Patient
Access to application	5	20	0	0
Access to levels screen	5	20	0	0
Select a level	4	16	1	4
Access to selected level interface	4	17	1	3
Execution of proposed exercise	4	15	1	5

tasks of software developed for medical therapies associated with dyslexia, it can be seen that the entrance to application and the access to levels was considered easy by 100% of respondents. In general terms, 76% of respondents determined that execution of the proposed exercise was easy.

A fourth instrument was designed to reflect contrast between different media that can be used as support tools for dyslexia therapies in Fig. 8, showing that a sample of 25 speech therapists have positively evaluated the use of television with respect to the most well-known media such as paper and the computer.

Question 4. According to your criteria and based on Ecuadorian context, in what percentage the following means should be used: paper, computer or television as a support to the dyslexia therapies (Table 6)?

Figure 8 shows that specialists consulted in their entirety agreed that no means should be exclusive when using it as a support for therapies, given that none of the three media were evaluated in more than 60% for their use. It is observed, moreover, that audiovisual media range from 1 to 60% in preferences of use, having a higher

Table 6. Results of assessment survey of user experience in use of means to perform the therapies

%	Paper	Computer	TV
0	7	0	0
1 a 20	10	5	5
21 a 40	3	10	13
41 a 60	5	10	7
61 a 80	0	0	0
81 a 100	0	0	0

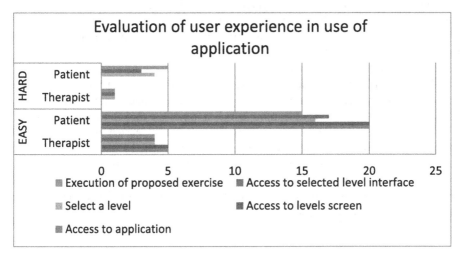

Fig. 7. Satisfaction of new equipment used in Medical Therapies

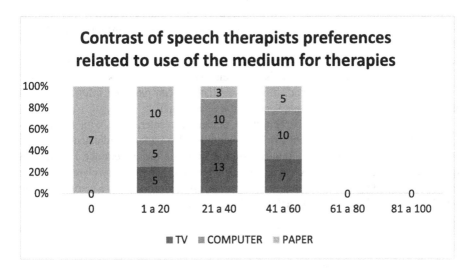

Fig. 8. Preference in use of medium to perform dyslexia therapies.

concentration between 20 and 60%, however, paper is still considered as a traditional medium, although its percentage of use is low, given that its highest concentration is between 0 and 20%.

6 Conclusions

The design of the solution displays a basic therapy aimed at patients with Developmental or Evolutionary Dyslexia registered in Medical Therapy Center of Medical Sciences Faculty of Universidad de Guayaquil, this therapy was proposed and supervised by speech therapists from Medical Technology School of Universidad de Guayaquil. The design can be configured in web environment of the tool and then converge as exercises to be developed by patients in therapeutic sessions. This convergence in environments allows taking pertinent actions to adapt therapies according to evolution of the patient.

The developed application is highly easy to use, focused on target population (children with dyslexia disorders), the use of remote control as an interface for the development of therapies and the consistency of navigation and buttons of interaction allowed patients to have a rapid learning curve in use of the tool and focus directly on development of therapy. The interface complies with the suggested guidelines for the creation of content and interaction with users, as provided by standards in digital terrestrial television. For the content of the therapies, the playful model has been applied with the inclusion of images according to the age of patients. In addition to distribution of contents, good visualization practices were considered to increase the ease of interaction with the patient.

7 Future Work

The vision in medium term is to have statistics of the values originated by the tool. These statistics should be defined or configured by the therapist in such a way that the values obtained be, posterior, a support for decision making regarding medical evolution from the patients.

The personalization of therapies for patients is another point to work in later developments, in this way the therapist can generate a medical work according to the evolution that the patient has had, this personalization can generate information that forms part of the statistics indicated in previous paragraph.

Evolution in the use of other interface devices for interaction with the tool is another point to consider in future work. The comfort that patients indicated to have in use of remote control, laid the foundations for study of the experience in terms of ergonomics and learning of new devices that encompass other sensory elements of the patient, such as 3D glasses, kinetic, touch screens, among others, these elements being considered in the future development of DTT applications.

References

1. Ministerio de Telecomunicaciones y de la Sociedad de la Información - Ecuador. https://www.telecomunicaciones.gob.ec/wp-content/uploads/downloads/2015/02/PRESENTACIO%CC%81N_TDT_MINTEL-Febrero-2015.pdfll
2. U. De and T. Digital, Libro de aplicaciones y usabilidad de la televisión digital interactiva: V Jornadas Iberoamericanas sobre Aplicaciones y Usabilidad de la Televisión Digital Interactiva, jAUTI2016. Artículos seleccionados (2016)
3. Abásolo, M., Castro, C.: Anales de jAUTI 2013 (2014)
4. C. Diagn, DSM-5
5. Franceschini, S., et al.: Action video games improve reading abilities and visual-to-auditory attentional shifting in English-speaking children with dyslexia. Sci. Rep. **7**(1), 1–12 (2017)
6. Tobolcea, I.: Computer-based Programs in Speech Therapy of Dyslalia and Dyslexia-Dysgraphia, pp. 52–63
7. Terapia de estimulación cognitiva cuando quieras, desde dónde quieras – Asociación Párkinson Madrid
8. Burlamaqui, A.M.F., et al.: Low Cost T-Health and T-Social with Ginga. In: Handbook of Research on ICTs for Human-Centered Healthcare and Social Care Services, October 2016, pp. 303–318 (2013)
9. Lorenzo, S.T.: Dyslexia and difficulties in acquisition of reading and writing skills, vol. 1, pp. 423–432 (2017)
10. Reid Lyon, G., et al.: PART I defining dyslexia, comorbidity, teachers' knowledge of language and reading a definition of dyslexia. Ann. Dyslexia Ann. Dyslexia **53** (1995)
11. Margarita Alba Gámez, J.G.C., Carlos Garrido Gil, P.M.L., Inmaculada Lorente Tortosa, J.P.M., Ma Montoro Victoria, Á., Ma José Rabadán Pardo, F.R.L.: Actualización en Dislexia del Desarrollo
12. García Mediavilla, J., Luis, C.M.G., de Quintanal Díaz, M.: La dislexia: características, diagnóstico, reeducación (2000)
13. Etchepareborda Simonini, M.C.: La intervención en los trastornos disléxicos: entrenamiento de la conciencia fonológica. Rev. Neurol. **36**(1), 13 (2003)
14. Song, J., Yang, Z., Wang, J.: Basic concepts of digital terrestrial television transmission system. Digit. Terr. Telev. Broadcast. 1–38 (2015)
15. Lessiter, J., Freeman, J., Dumbreck, A.: Understanding DTT remote control button labelling: a multi-method approach. In: euroITV 2004, May 2014
16. Tscheligi, M., Obrist, M., Lugmayr, A. (eds.): EuroITV 2008. LNCS, vol. 5066. Springer, Heidelberg (2008). https://doi.org/10.1007/978-3-540-69478-6
17. D. Tv, G. Nine, and E. Lane, UK Digital TV Receiver Recommendations, vol. 44, pp. 1–34, May 2010
18. EiTV smartBox|EiTV. https://www.eitv.com.br/es/produtos/eitv-smartbox/. Accessed 17 June 2018
19. Standardization Sector and ITU: ITU-T, vol. 761 (2014)
20. inicio|Ginga. http://www.ginga.org.br/es. Accessed 12 June 2018
21. Normas Brasileiras de TV Digital. http://forumsbtvd.org.br/index.php/normas-brasileiras-de-tv-digital. Accessed 13 June 2018

22. Soares, L.F.G., Rodrigues, R.F., Moreno, M.F.: Ginga-NCL: the declarative environment of the Brazilian digital TV system. J. Brazilian Comput. Soc. **13**(1), 37–46 (2007)
23. Organization Ginga: Ginga (2012)
24. Soares, L.F.G., Barbosa, S.D.J.: Programando em NCL 3.0, Desenvolv. Apl. para o Middlew. Ginga, pp. 1–589 (2009)
25. Lua, R.I.: Programming in Lua, 1st edn. December 2003 (2004)

Integrated Wireless Prototype with Monitoring Applications to Measure Water Quality in Shrimp Farms

Renato Conforme[✉][iD], Roberto Crespo[✉], María Argüello-Vélez[✉],
Maria Fernanda Molina-Miranda[✉][iD], and Ericka Yanez[✉][iD]

Universidad de Guayaquil, Guayaquil, Ecuador
renato.conforme.rosado@gmail.com,
{roberto.crespom,maria.arguellove,maria.molinam}@ug.edu.ec,
erickayc11@hotmail.com

Abstract. In shrimp farming, ponds or pools are considered the habitat where shrimp grow and develop. In this ecosystem, shrimp are affected by biochemical, climate agents and deficient maintenance. Those situations cause diseases, death of the species and eventually monetary losses to the aquaculture industry. To face this problem, a monitoring system for shrimp pools is proposed. The system will be constructed with wireless technology and sensors to monitor the main physico-chemical parameters in the shrimp farming process. This proposal aims to contribute saving resources that are involved in the processes of shrimp farming as well as meeting the need to remotely obtain real time information, allowing to make critical decisions and ensuring optimal harvest with minimum losses.

Keywords: Arduino · Monitoring system · Wireless technology ·
Physico-chemical parameters · ESP8266 · Shrimp farms

1 Introduction

Ecuador is a country that has a high development potential in a wide variety of industries. One of those industries is aquaculture where shrimp cultivation and harvest constitute one of the most outstanding activities in this productive sector. To carry out this activity, shrimp producers face prevalent circumstances that directly affect the growth process of shrimp in farming. The main circumstance is the deterioration of water quality in the ponds [1]. Ponds situation is affected by climate changes, use of excessive chemical agents and deficiency in maintenance. Therefore it is necessary to monitor and control the physico-chemical parameters that influence water quality.

Ponds state depends on the variation of different indicators to guarantee a good harvest [2]. According to [3], temperature, water level, amount of dissolved oxygen, pH level, turbidity, salinity, change of color and alkalinity are some

© Springer Nature Switzerland AG 2019
M. Botto-Tobar et al. (Eds.): ICCCE 2018, CCIS 959, pp. 31–42, 2019.
https://doi.org/10.1007/978-3-030-12018-4_3

parameters used to define and measure water quality. Dissolved oxygen is a very important individual variable that depends on water temperature in the pond. When the temperature reaches high levels it can cause the shellfish dead. On the other hand, pH indicates the acidity level of water that determines whether physical or biological changes have occurred in the shrimp habitat [4]. Therefore, dissolved oxygen, temperature, and pH were chosen as the most critical parameters for the proposed system [5]. These parameters should reach values ranges shown in Table 1 to shrimp grow and develop under optimal conditions.

Table 1. Water quality norm values*[3] [4] [5]

Parameters	Normal value range
pH (normed units)	6.0–9.5
Dissolved oxygen (mg/L)	5.0–15.0
Temperature (°C)	22–30

This study proposes a design of a wireless system applicable to the constant monitoring of shrimp habitat, resulting in a prototype that allows demonstrating the functional management and the benefits of monitoring the parameters in a pond.

2 Problem Statement

The shrimp producer is responsible for extensive areas of land that are used for the creation of the ponds where shrimp are grown and harvested. For this reason, the personnel in charge of the collection of water samples travel great distances to obtain the necessary data for the analysis. This influences the efficiency of the periodic and simultaneous monitoring of the development of this kind of shellfish. Additionally, the physico-chemical parameters manually collected are exposed to human mistakes, which can lead to erroneous results. This process, added to the manual handling of pumps and motors that oxygenate and control the water level, can generate serious consequences in the yield of the shrimp production.

Posing an ideal scenario, only shrimp farms with sufficient economic capacity can use vehicles and hire the necessary personnel to cover pond monitoring on a regular basis. Also, the same employees should cover preventive and corrective maintenance. However, this does not occur in practice. As a result of the above-mentioned deficiencies, shrimp gets stressed out which causes lack of hunger, disease, death and therefore a decrease in total production. The direct cause of this problem is normally poor conditions in the ponds which can be caused by one of the following:

- Poor preventive maintenance.
- Lack of constant control of each parameter.
- Delayed corrective maintenance.

3   Background

The integration of mobile devices, the Internet, and wireless connectivity offer mobility that provides an opportunity for entities in general to extend their information and services. Proper planning can increase productivity, reduce operating costs and increase customer satisfaction. "Wireless LANs offer many advantages over conventional Ethernet LANs (wired networks), such as mobility, flexibility, scalability, speed, simplicity and reduced installation costs" [6].

In the aquaculture sector, there are different technological solutions at all levels of production. The company Apracom S.A. is a solution provider for the aquaculture industry located in Guayas, Ecuador. One of their star products is an automatic feeding system for shrimp using AQ1 system. This system, by means of sensors, detects the presence of shrimp and feeds them automatically. These feeding cycles are sent to a web service which stores them in a database. All this connectivity is done with a wireless infrastructure.

The technical manager of the company affirms that "the problems regarding distance and time in covering all the shrimp farm has always been an overlooked issue" [7]. From the beginning of AQ1 System operations in Ecuador, aquaculture sector has overcome resistance related to implementing wireless technology to production processes. The manager also says "the use of wireless technology applied to a monitoring system is a real advantage, using the resources efficiently and optimizing response times in adverse situations" [7].

4   Technological Solution

When samples of physico-chemical parameters are obtained manually, the development of shrimps is affected by dispersed values. For this reason, the optimal conditions where the shrimp is fully developed have been evaluated and prototyped so it will allow the biologists or personnel in charge to carry out constant monitoring to reduce the mortality rate of the shrimp is proposed [8].

The design of this prototype is build upon an Arduino-Uno module with three sensors, one for each parameter. In this study, the following aspects have been considered: dissolved oxygen, pH, and temperature. In addition, a wireless component is integrated into the system. The wireless component allow all communication between sensors and the web application. Finally, the measured values of the three parameters are captured, transmitted and processed [9].

4.1   Monitoring System Proposal

The prototype is structured by several modules with different technologies and for this reason, the modules have been developed independently, these are: scanning, processing, storage, and accessing module. The modules are communicated between one another through a compound wired - wireless local network. In Fig. 1 the indicated structure is presented.

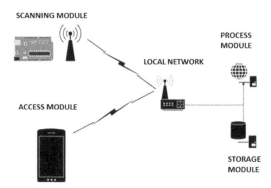

Fig. 1. Structure of the monitoring system

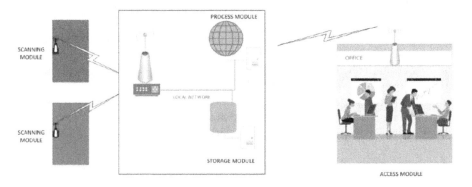

Fig. 2. Diagram of the physical location of the monitoring system

Physical Location of Modules. Scanning module, which is represented by an antenna in Fig. 2, is in each pool to monitor water quality. A closer sight of it is shown in Fig. 3 where the sensor of the scanning module must be submerged in the water to do an effective data collection. The process and storage modules according to the company policies and resources must be housed a single team or a dedicated team for each module. Regardless of the case, it is located with the access point to the local network, all in the same physical space. The access module does not have a fixed location. It provides mobility for the user since it is an application hosted on a mobile device with access to the local network via wireless. The only condition is that it is located within the coverage area of the access point to the local network.

4.2 Functionality of Modules

– Scanning module - This module is made up of Arduino Uno module integrated with an oxygen sensor, a temperature sensor, a pH sensor and a radio transmission card. Its function is to record information obtained from sensors

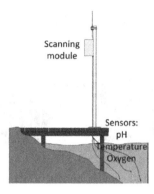

Scanning
module

Sensors:
pH
Temperature
Oxygen

Fig. 3. Physical location of the scanning module

when they are in contact with water in the ponds. This data will be transmitted through the wireless network to the next module named processing module.

- Processing module - Local web service processes data as follows: it waits for the POST request to obtain the Arduino-UNO module frame, then it defrags the frame to extract the information from the measurements of the parameters. After this, it has to send it to next module, storage module. Process module also has more functions, which are to query data registered, useful for "access module", and to validate login page for applications.
- Storage module - Properly, it is the database where information obtained from scanning module will be stored, as well as date and time of each record, in order to obtain a history of measurements, and to generate reports.
- Access Module - It consists of two applications, a mobile and a web application that allow users to consult current values of three parameters: dissolved oxygen, hydrogen potential, and temperature. Data is obtained from processing module and is updated automatically. To gain access to this module it is required username and password. Those are validated by processing module, then the application makes a query to the service which shows measurements of the parameters. This process is repeated every period of time automatically in order to present updated values. When measured values are beyond tolerable limits, application issues a notification alerting user about it a proper decisions can be made.

This design is focused on scanning module which is built on an Arduino Uno board that has some advantages such as its low cost and its configurable feature because is open-source based. Arduino Uno is responsible for containing and executing instructions that allow reading of physico-chemical parameters obtained by sensors. In addition, it converts information into a single frame that is sent to processing module through ESP8266 WiFi module.

ESP8266 is a WiFi module configured through AT commands by implementing a serial to USB adapter (see Fig. 4), allowing a direct configuration with the

AT commands or with Arduino. In both cases, configuration is valid to have access to local network.

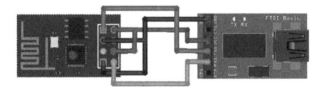

Fig. 4. Serial connection with USB adapter

Figure 5 shows connection between ESP8266 module and Arduino UNO module. These steps are required to configure it:

1. To enable connection with local network - ESP8266 module is reset, SSID and password are sent as response to connection request and then connection is confirmed.
2. To enable reception of registered values - IP address and port of protocol (TCP/UDP) type to be used are configured, then a request in HTTP protocol format is built, in which request type (GET/POST), service location in server that attends the request, IP address of the server and frame that has values of parameters are contained.

This process is repeated constantly in order to keep service up-to-date with changes in physico-chemical parameters of the pond.

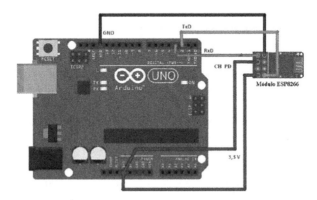

Fig. 5. Connection of ESP8266 module to Arduino UNO module

Connection Between ESP8266 Module and Arduino UNO Module.
The variable "esp", which represents a serial connection, is initialized. It is declared as follows:

```
SoftwareSerial esp(3, 2);
```

The values three and two represent the data reception and transmission pins of the Arduino UNO board respectively. These are connected to the module ESP8266. Then the number of bauds to transmit between Arduino UNO and module ESP8266 is indicated.

```
void setup()
{
esp.begin(115200);
}
```

After that, the module is reset.

```
esp.println("AT+RST");
```

Then, SSID and password of WiFi is sent:

```
esp.println("AT + CWJAP=\"" + ssid +"\",\"" + password + "\"");
```

The route is started by configuring type of transport protocol, the server's IP address and the port to establish the connection.

```
esp.println("AT + CIPSTART = \"TCP\",\"" + server + "\",80");
```

The structure of the POST request is formed by the server path to which the request is going to be sent (url), the IP address of the server (server), the length of the frame (data.length) and the content of the frame (data).

```
String postRequest =
"POST " + uri + " HTTP/1.0\r\n" +
"Host: " + server + "\r\n" +
"Accept: *" + "/" + "*\r\n" +
"Content-Length: " + data.length() + "\r\n" +
"Content-Type: application/x-www-form-urlencoded\r\n" +
"\r\n" + data;
```

The request is sent with the corresponding AT command.

```
esp.print("AT + CIPSEND = ");
esp.println(postRequest.length() );
```

Finally, it is validated with an answer, then the route is closed.

```
esp.println("AT + CIPCLOSE");
```

User Interfaces. To expose integral accessibility by applying wireless technology, two applications were developed to provide access to information provided by senders, these are stored in a database. Both applications have an user-friendly interface that makes it easier to operate and intuitive.

Web Application. Web application is part of Access and Process Module, it is composed of two sections: operation and presentation. Next, a brief description:

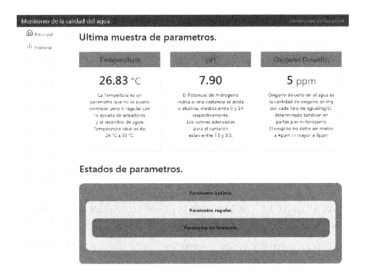

Fig. 6. Main screenshot of the web application (Color figure online)

Operation. It includes functions that allow storage of information from sensors in Arduino to database. This module is transparent to user.

Presentation. From this module, stored information in database is presented and it has two screens that can be viewed from a browser.

The main screenshot (see Fig. 6) shows last record of three parameters obtained from database with assigned concepts and ranges. At the bottom of the screen-shot is a defined color palette which determines state of parameter indicating if it is optimum with blue color, regular with yellow color or not tolerable with red color.

Figure 7 shows history screenshot with tables of each parameter with a finite number of samples obtained from actual day, this allows us to know variation of parameters over a day.

Mobile App. The mobile application is part of the access module, it can be accessed from a Smartphone with an Android operating system, it was developed with the intention of having access from any point within the coverage area of the

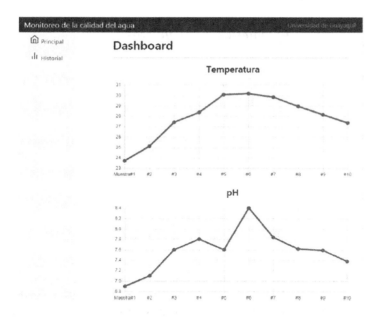

Fig. 7. Parameter history screenshot

wireless network. Facilitating this way, the mobility of the user, at the same time allowing the monitoring of the quality of the water and alerting with notifications when the parameters are out-side the tolerated values. This application has two screens: The initial screen prevents the access of users not registered by the administrator, you need to sign in with an authorized user and password, see Fig. 8.

Fig. 8. Login screen in the mobile application

The Fig. 9 displays the last record of the three parameters obtained from the data-base. It has an "UPDATE" button that clears the text boxes corresponding to the values of the three parameters and has the last value obtained by the scanning module.

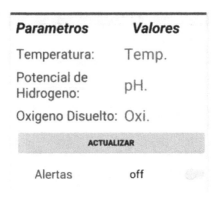

Fig. 9. Parameter display screen

Database. For the operation of the prototype, the monitoring system requires a database that stores the values of each of the parameters into a single record, adding the date and time. For the identification of each scanning module, it also has a field that keeps a unique code for each module (Fig. 10).

Fig. 10. Database administration interface

5   Conclusions and Recommendations

5.1   Conclusions

The most relevant parameters for the right development of shrimp in shrimp farms depend on parameters such as dissolved oxygen, pH and temperature. For this reason, these parameters are being considered for the analysis and design of the prototype. The measurement of the parameters is given qualitatively in real time allowing to the employee access from any location that is within the radius of coverage. The system recognizes when it is necessary to manipulate the physico-chemical parameters to reduce the reduction of shrimp production.

Finally, it is concluded that integrating the reading of several sensors in a module and the fact that their connectivity is wireless, greatly serve the need of reducing costs. Also, accessing the information live is allowed through the same local network by connecting a mobile device to the Access point minimizing response times outright.

5.2 Recommendations

Three parameters studied to measure water quality index of shrimp farms are not the only relevant measures to be collected. It is recommended to adapt additional sensors for more detailed implementation cases. In case of the number of parameters exceeds capacity of Arduino UNO, it must be replaced by an Arduino with more capacity, such as; Arduino MEGA.

Because power lines do not reach all pools, it is likely that the system can not be installed in all of them because there is no access to a power source. Considering the scanning module is of low consumption, it is recommended the analysis and design of the adaptation of a self-sustaining system with solar panels as a power source and batteries for the night feeding.

It is recommended to analyze the acquisition of more powerful wireless devices so that mobility is not limited by radius of coverage of the devices. Since the scanning module is a static device, it is suggested to use directional antennas pointed to the access point to cover greater distances.

References

1. AQUA Cultura, edición # 93 by REVISTA AQUACULTURA - Cámara Nacional de Acuacultura - issuu (n.d.). https://issuu.com/revista-cna/docs/aqua_cultura_93/34. Accessed 6 Oct 2018
2. Rojas, Haws, Cabanillas (n.d.): Buenas Prácticas de Manejo Para el Cultivo de Camarón. https://www.crc.uri.edu/download/PKD_good_mgt_field_manual.pdf
3. Boyd, C.E.: Management practices for reducing the environmental impacts of shrimp farming. In: Methods for Improving Shrimp Farming in Central America, pp. 261–292 (2001)
4. Ramírez Mora, A.G. (n.d.): Evaluación y determinación de la calidad del agua en las piscinas de la camaronera Boca Salima, para el mejoramiento de la producción de Camarón. Loja, Ecuador (2015)
5. Vides (n.d.): Parámetros Físico Químico_Acuícultura Hoy. http://consideraciones-acuicolas2.webnode.com.co/news/parametros-fisico-quimicos/. Accessed 6 Oct 2018
6. Ramírez, J., Díaz, J.V.: Las redes inalámbricas, más ventajas que desventajas. Ciencia Administrativa, vol. 2 (2008). https://www.uv.mx/iiesca/files/2012/12/redes2008-2.pdf
7. Conforme Rosado, R.L., Meza Cercado, C.I.: Análisis y diseño de la aplicación de las redes inalámbricas en un sistema de monitoreo del habitat del camarón para las camaroneras del Guayas. Guayaquil, Ecuador (2018)

8. Laguarda, Garcia, C.: Control y supervisión mediante un sistema microcontrolador de los parámetros de calidad de agua de un estanque. Universidad de Sevilla (2017). http://bibing.us.es/proyectos/abreproy/91103/fichero/TFG-AntonioPerezFinal.pdf

9. Bórquez-López, R.A., et al.: Monitoreo Del Índice De Calidad Del Agua Para Camaronicultura Por Medio De Un Hardware De Acceso Abierto Y Un Sistema De Inferencia Difusa. Revista de Ciencias Biológicas y de La Salud **19**(3), 45–49 (2016). https://biotecnia.unison.mx/index.php/biotecnia/article/view/449

10. Vaca Simbala, R.D.: Implementación de Interfaz electrónica para la medición y registro de temperatura en una piscina camaronera mediante aplicación Web. Machala (2015). http://repositorio.utmachala.edu.ec/handle/48000/5034

11. Lledó, E., Sáez Barona, S., Atienza Vanacloig, V.: Diseño de un sistema de control domótico basado en la plataforma Arduino. Universitat Politècnica de València (2012). https://riunet.upv.es/bitstream/handle/10251/18228/Memoria.pdf

12. Crespo, E.: Entorno de Programación de Arduino (IDE) — Aprendiendo Arduino (2016). https://aprendiendoarduino.wordpress.com/2016/03/29/entorno-de-programacion-de-arduino-ide/. Accessed 6 Oct 2018

13. Pradillo, B.: Parámetros de control del agua potable (2016). https://www.iagua.es/blogs/beatriz-pradillo/parametros-control-agua-potable. Accessed 6 Oct 2018

Real Time Automatic Andon Alerts for Android Platforms Applied in Footwear Manufacturing

John Reyes[1(✉)], Luis Morales[1], Darwin Aldas[1], Renato Reyes[2],
and Renato Toasa[1,3]

[1] Universidad Técnica de Ambato, Ambato, Tungurahua, Ecuador
{johnpreyes,luisamorales,darwinsaldas,
rtoasa4167}@uta.edu.ec
[2] Universidad Técnica Particular de Loja, Loja, Ecuador
crreyes5@utpl.edu.ec
[3] Universidad Tecnológica Israel, Quito, Ecuador
rtoasa@uisrael.edu.ec

Abstract. In recent years, there has been a substantial technological improvement in industrial control rooms that monitor manufacturing processes. Real-time systems for monitoring in traditional production are static since they are handled from an office. For this reason it is very important to develop a mobile application that allows capturing and visualizing information in different company areas in a dynamic way. The objective of this research is to develop an industrial software module based on the Andon System oriented to footwear industry that consists of an Android mobile application that consumes the information managed in the planning and production programming modules. The module has a website that monitors in real time the status of the industrial facility and the progress of scheduling based on lean manufacturing techniques for notification, emission and visualization of unscheduling stoppages presented during production. The experimental results show that the module is adaptable in the production processes, delivering timely notifications and projecting an efficiency of 95% in the production process after 38 successful experiments.

Keywords: Alerts · Android · Web · Andon · Real-time · Footwear · Enterprise

1 Introduction

Large, small and medium industries have been evolving towards a systematic change in their manufacturing management trying to find successful methods for excellent production planning and control [1].

The footwear industry is expanding rapidly; according to the Global Footwear Market Analysis published by Global Footwear Market 2017–2021, the total revenues of the global footwear market in the past two years were 258.5 billion dollars which represented an annual compound growth rate of 4.4% between 2012 and 2016. The value in footwear production is expected to increase in the coming years [2]. Most companies

© Springer Nature Switzerland AG 2019
M. Botto-Tobar et al. (Eds.): ICCCE 2018, CCIS 959, pp. 43–56, 2019.
https://doi.org/10.1007/978-3-030-12018-4_4

that are in the manufacturing sector face systematic problems in the production processes and to solve it there are certain tools derived from lean manufacturing. Among these tools is the Andon system, although something simple, it is a system that deep inside has a great benefit: building a higher product quality in the processes or operations in which there are critical points, thus being a necessary tool for any company that has a continuous production line so that this increases its productivity and quality, and can grow in the industry [3]. In addition, it seeks to implement a successful and lasting improvement process. Over time, many industries have identified and documented the best operational practices to meet their specific production objectives. Production scheduling has become a challenge [4].

The key to the success or failure of a manufacturing company depends on good planning and the use of production systems such as Lean Manufacturing (LM). This methodology presents its tool called Andon, which allows to show notifications or alerts about abnormal events in production in real time [1]. With this, the industries are able to quickly and efficiently manage the interruptions generated, thereby optimizing resources and reducing downtime [5].

Companies, in general, expect that their productive operation is in accordance with the planned avoiding waste in processes. In this way, the implementation of the logic of the Andon System which is a visual management tool used in the Toyota Production System has great importance to obtain competitive advantages in the management of supply chain [6]. In relation to mobile web applications that today are one of the best forms of social interaction, and is expected to grow significantly year after year by doubling the number of users and their time spent on them [7], the adoption of smartphones continues spreading across society since most people in the world have a smartphone [8]. People depend more and more on their mobile phones to send and receive messages, notifications and alerts in real time [9]. In this context, making use of computer tools allows agile decision-making and calculations to optimize resources and improve processes. This work develops an Industrial Module that consists of 2 parts: first, the development of a mobile application for devices with Android operating system that aims at using the characteristics of the Andon System focused on the use of lean manufacturing techniques for the notification, emission and visualization of information, all this for the operational optimization in the production of footwear industries; the second part is to develop a web application that allows to visualize and process the information stored by the mobile application – this process is done in real time. In addition to this, experimentation is formalized and, using learning curves, the developed module is validated. The main objective of this research is to optimize production systems, minimizing waste and damage; these logistical improvements will provide better productivity. In this way it is possible to solve the problem of delay in production processes due to the lack of timely alerts.

The article is organized as follows: Sect. 2 presents the Contextualization and literature review for this research, Sect. 3 presents the case study on which the research is developed, while the information on the industrial module is presented in Sect. 4, Sect. 5 mentions real-time communication, integration with Enterprise Resource Planning (ERP) is shown in Sect. 6, the experimental results are presented in Sect. 7 and, finally, the conclusions are detailed in Sect. 8.

2   Contextualization and Literature Review

Mobile devices have revolutionized the entire world; part of this important global trend has involved changing the way people communicate with each other [7]. One of the elements of this change has been real-time applications that are commonly used to monitor and control the dynamics of underlying physical processes in many applications. Their objective is to improve the performance, reliability and security of applications [10] since this type of applications are widely used by companies to show how their processes are performed and optimized; real-time applications improve the processes of enabled systems with Graphics Processing Unit (GPU) [11].

In the same way, footwear industries have been improving their processes using computer systems such as alert systems, which in most cases are limited to being static desktop systems that cause not timely alerts in the processes of the footwear industries. Andon is a system used to alert problems in production processes, these alerts are made using color codes. For example, yellow is used in production failures; quality in blue; materials in green and maintenance in red [12]. There are few industries and companies that use Andon systems and there are currently few reports of use of Andon Systems, based on mobile platforms. The search for articles on this topic has proved unsuccessful, but a broader search helped to find cases of the use of Andon Systems in companies. The famous Toyota car company applies the successful mechanism (Andon-Cord) to software development process along the entire production line of vehicles [13]. In the assembly line, the product passes from one worker to another, so all the processes will be carried out sequentially. Through the experiments carried out by Toyota, a 90% decrease in waste is obtained and a saving of $474,149.76, in an optimistic scenario [14]. That's why the Andon-Cord mechanism is so successful at Toyota. In Ecuador, a study that refers to the importance of the implementation of the Andon System in a vehicle assembly company was carried out, with the objective of collaborating with one of three fundamental concepts of Kaizen, which is the mitigation and elimination of waste [14]. An Andon wireless system based on Zigbee has also been made. This system performs the wireless transmission of Andon's information on special construction lines and has some functions that include production monitoring, wireless calls and statistics reporting [15]. ZigBee's radio frequency technology is adopted by the system to perform wireless communication. The implementation of this system allows to provide valuable data on production losses in each process within the assembly line separately, and to calculate key performance indicators of these areas and as a whole [14].

Finally, to validate that the developed module facilitates the production processes in the footwear industries, a learning curve is used, which is a line that shows the relationship between the production time of a unit and the accumulated number of units produced. The theory of the learning curve has multiple applications in the business world; in the case of manufacturing, it calculates the time it takes to design and produce a product [16].

3   Case Study

This research is a complement of a research project that develops an ERP called Footwear Advanced Planning and Scheduling System (FAPS), this system is a complete and complex software architecture with different web technologies [4] and it is improved by adding the module of this paper.

Production planning of the system (FAPS) is based on products, with the operation model called "make to order" and during the production day a mix of products is manufacturing for the variety of models that are offered to the market. The industrial module developed in this research integrates information on manufacturing and failures from all processes in real time to generate indicators that allow taking corrective decisions. The wireless connection interface offers flexibility for the mobility of Android devices throughout the entire industrial installation. The web system is in the information boards, and it allows to visualize the alerts of failures and advance planning to all staff to accelerate the cycle time and meet the set objectives, in working day.

The footwear production process has three main macro processes: die-cutting, sewing and assembly. In the cutting process, a specific material is cut by a sharp steel die, which gives shape to it; the sewing process deals with the task of joining the cuts or pieces obtained in the punching process and, finally, the assembly process prepares the cut and adjusts it to a last shape of shoe [12].

Shoe manufacturing industries usually exhibit repetitive processes in manufacturing. The work cycle is based on a batch production method, which applies the separation of operations for the completion of the final product. The processes for footwear manufacturing within the industrial environment meet the requirements for the implementation and development of the industrial module.

3.1   Development Considerations

First, the main processes that lead the manufacture of footwear are defined: Die-cutting, Fitting and Assembly. Next, it is determined that the fitting process is the one that generates a delay in production. The defects and abnormalities that have arisen prior to the application of the tool are low quality products, machine failures, defective materials and delays due to machinery maintenance.

When identifying possible abnormalities in the production process it is essential to determine a color code for each of them in order to optimize the response times of the recognition of these abnormalities. Otherwise, an efficiency of the time required will not be achieved and it will be possible to see unscheduling stoppages in the production. Table 1 shows the color code, depending on the process.

Table 1. Code color per process.

Process	Color code
Quality	Blue
Materials	Green
Maintenance	Red

After having selected the critical processes with their respective color codes, the industrial module developed to perform the pilot tests is implemented whose aims is measuring response times for abnormal situations within a working day.

The experiment was carried out in a footwear company belonging to the National Chamber of Footwear of Tungurahua (CALTU) in Ecuador, using as parameters in quantity: 6 units of footwear per size; in sizes 39, 40, 41, shoe type is industrial safety and; these experiments were carried out on different days with different times, with the objective of determining the production efficiency of this footwear company – this is detailed in the Test and Results chapter.

4 Industrial Module

The general scheme of the industrial module developed in this research consists of a web application and a mobile application for Android platforms (see Fig. 1). The web application and the mobile application use a web server and a database server. In the web server, the corresponding web services are published for information management and, in the database server, this information is stored. The mobile application collects the information in real time while the web application displays this information: if a strange error occurs, an alert occurs.

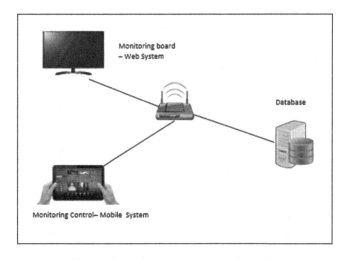

Fig. 1. General scheme – industrial module

Table 2. Mobile system functionality

Specification	Description
Name	Production management and alerts
Actors	Worker
Pre-conditions	Both user and mobile device information must be stored on the database
Normal flow	The system requires a username and password
	The system validates the information
	The system verifies the user's permissions
	The system enables the production monitoring and alert management module
Alternative flow	The user have not the necessary permissions to access the functions of the mobile application or there are no planned orders for their current permissions
Future conditions	The system sends the production status to the database server

Table 3. Web system functionality

Specification	Description
Name	Production and alerts monitoring
Actors	Manager
Pre-conditions	User information must be stored on the database and production orders must be previously planned for the current day and shift
Normal flow	The system requires a username and password
	The system validates the information
	The system verifies the user's permissions
	The user selects the process and the production line to be monitored
Alternative flow	There are no planned orders with the parameters previously selected to be monitored
Future conditions	When the user finds a problem or a failure in the production process, it must be solved

The database server contains the information of the scheduling shoe production orders, which will be sent through the web services to a mobile application for the corresponding notification of a new pair or a fault found during the production process within a working day. The web system shows in real time the status of the production and their efficiency, in addition to the possible failures issued by the mobile application for immediate solution. After this, it is necessary to define the functionality of the industrial module; the following tables (Tables 2 and 3) detail the functionality of the mobile system and the web system.

5   Real Time Communication

According to the real demands, the system requires a reliable network, therefore, we opted for a wireless network, which uses the Protocol Address Resolution Protocol (ARP) for sending information. It is collected by mobile devices and sent to the server, thus generating alerts in the shoe production process. The ARP protocol plays an important role among communication protocols related to Transmission Control Protocol/Internet Protocol (TCP/IP). The communication is done on an own network with an own router, which guarantees that there is no loss of data.

Its main objective is to know the physical address Media Access Control (MAC) of a network interface card corresponding to an IP address. That's where his name comes from: Address resolution protocol [17] (see Fig. 2). Each device connected to a network has a 48-bit number (6 hexadecimal blocks of 8 bits each) that identifies it. This address is unique for each device. The first 24 bits identify the manufacturer and the last 24 are those of the equipment. It is said equipment because it can be a computer, tablet, smartphone, arduino, raspberry, etc. Internet communication does not directly use this address (MAC), but uses IP addresses, i.e., there must be a relationship between physical and logical addresses. The following figure shows how communication is performed.

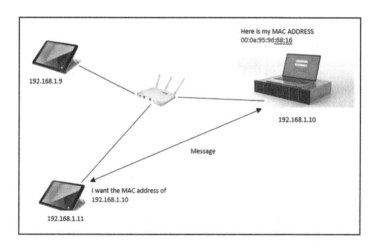

Fig. 2. Communication through ARP protocol

6 Module Integration with Enterprise Resource Planning (ERP)

Figure 3 presents the architecture of the ERP called FAPS, reflecting the internal modules such as: planning and programming (customers, orders and products), process management and the module corresponding to manufacturing management/notification (Andon) which is the one mentioned in this article. To integrate these modules, the design is complemented with a database in charge of storing all the information that is generated in the FAPS System. The storage and management of data is done with the Database Management System (SGBD) PostgreSQL 9.5 [18], on a Windows server platform. For the design of the Relationship Entity Model (MER), static and dynamic data useful for the execution of the application were contemplated.

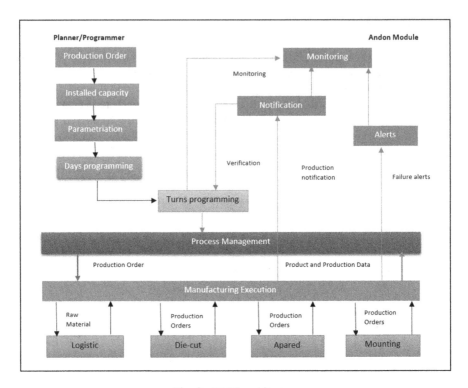

Fig. 3. FAPS architecture

FAPS is responsible for the management and planning of shoe production orders. Within the planning module the production order is distributed in number of days and shifts depending on the workload. The Andon module reflects the planned production in a working day for its proper notification of peers, in addition to the management of alerts in time, in terms of failures or problems encountered in the shoe production process. Through the information generated by the computer systems working together, reports of the efficiency produced in the execution of planned production orders are obtained.

7   Test and Results

The industrial module has two complementary modules: the first is dedicated to the production notification while the second focuses on monitoring unplanned machine shutdowns that occur during the workday. From the notification module, the planned order will be displayed next to its different models and sizes, the operator must select the model and the size to be produced using a button to add each produced pair (see Fig. 4).

Fig. 4. Notification screen

In the unplanned tracking module, 4 buttons are shown, which are assigned to the different types of abnormalities that may occur during the production process, which are: Production, Materials, Maintenance and Quality.

When issuing an alert internally, a timer is started until the person in charge of resolving the abnormalities within the production arrives at the workstation where the alert was issued by measuring the average reaction time, another counter is started to record the time means to repair that ends the moment the manager finishes making the corrections or maintenance to the machinery or raw material; this will depend on the alert that is issued.

The compliance review on production is done through a complementary screen of the Module (see Fig. 5), which indicates the number of pairs produced with respect to the planned quantity; in addition the screen allows to visualize the warnings for faults that are generated during the shift becoming an important tool for both supervisors and plant managers.

After doing the experiments in a footwear factory, the module generates a series of reports showing the date, the start and end time of the order and the efficiency based on the time the process took; the expected time it is shown in Table 4 and the real times in Table 5.

With the data of experimentation, the efficiency of each of the processes was calculated. Efficiency is a ratio between the actual production of a process and a given parameter [16]. These data are shown in Table 6.

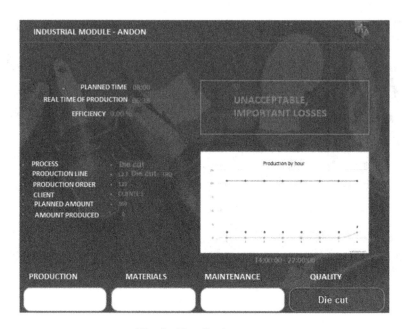

Fig. 5. Visualization screen

Table 4. Estimated times

Date	Expected time Die-cutting (H)	Expected time Fitting (H)	Expected time Assembly (H)
11/11/2017	1.41	1.6	1.05
25/11/2017	1.41	1.61	1.05
02/12/2017	1.41	1.61	1.05
09/12/2017	1.41	1.61	1.05
16/12/2017	1.41	1.61	1.05

Table 5. Real times

Date	Expected time Die-cutting (H)	Expected time Fitting (H)	Expected time Assembly (H)
11/11/2017	1.80	2.10	1.75
25/11/2017	1.78	2.47	1.49
02/12/2017	1.92	2.68	1.30
09/12/2017	1.72	2.07	1.41
16/12/2017	1.82	2.13	1.11

Table 6. Production process efficiency

Die-cutting efficiency (%)	Fitting efficiency (%)	Assembly efficiency (%)	Average efficiency (%)
78.33	76.19	60.00	71.51
79.24	65.12	70.36	71.57
73.54	60.15	80.76	71.48
81.96	77.89	74.44	78.10
77.50	75.63	94.19	82.44

To validate the module, the number of procedures necessary for efficient production has been determined. Learning curves are used, taking the actual times and estimates of die-cutting, fitting, and assembly. The calculation of the learning curve is made with Eq. (1), where Ym is the search time of the system, k is the time of the first experiment, x is the number of experiments and n is the logarithm of the percentage of learning that is obtained with Eq. (2), where b is the percentage of learning.

$$Ym = kx^n \tag{1}$$

$$N = \log b / \log \tag{2}$$

After the analysis, the number of necessary experiments is generated Table 7:

Table 7. Learning curve – analysis results

Required experiments Die-cutting	Required experiments Fitting	Required experiments Assembly	Required experiments total
27.11	39.44	53.72	37.60

Learning is the improvement resulting from people repeating a process and acquiring skill or efficiency based on their own experience. The analyses indicate that it takes about 38 experiments to achieve a 95% learning that is the average in this area of production [16], which would represent the company manufacturing 684 pairs.

The data was analysed in Matlab, version R2015a (8.5.0.197613), which is a high-performance technical calculation software for numerical calculation and visualization [19], this software generated the general learning curve of the process (see Fig. 6).

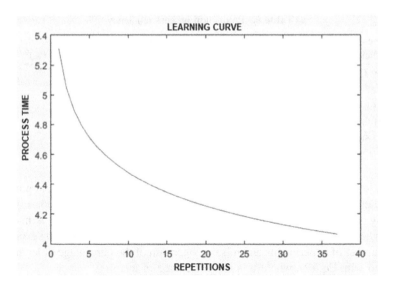

Fig. 6. Matlab generated learning curve

8   Conclusions

The implementation of the industrial computer control and monitoring module based on the Andon control system optimizes the performance of processes in shoe production environments since it minimizes response times to failures produced during the working day and allows to maintain a real-time control of the production process, allowing the timely detection of problems or inconveniences. Shorten downtime due to an immediate reaction giving solution to the problems that arise.

Real-time communication using the ARP protocol allows the company's employees to interact repeatedly with their physical working environment, by generating timely alerts, allowing immediate responses to failures generated in production.

Through the learning curve, the industrial module was validated, identifying that 38 production experiments will be necessary to obtain an efficiency of 95% and without losses in production, thus allowing footwear industries to optimize their processes and resources through timely alerts.

Acknowledgment. The authors thank the National Footwear Chamber of Ecuador and Technical University of Ambato (UTA) for the support provided during the execution of this work within the framework of the research project called "Operational optimization based on a lean dynamic system of alert of failures in the production processes for the footwear industry.

References

1. Kotwal, A., Dhami, S., Singh, S.: Evaluation of machine downtime and failure analysis of components in paint manufacturing unit: review paper. Int. J. Mech. Ind. Technol. **3**, 170–174 (2015)
2. Global Information, Inc.: Apparel and footwear global industry overview (2017). https://www.giiresearch.com/report/eo518847-apparel-footwear-globalindustry-overview.html
3. Administración de la producción: Sistema Andon. Andon (2014). http://andon2013.blogspot.com/2013/11/conclusiones.html
4. Reyes, J., et al.: Faps system: a prototype for lean manufacturing scheduling in footwear. In: XII Jornadas Iberoamericanas de Ingeniería de Software e Ingeniería del Conocimiento y Congreso Ecuatoriano en Ingeniería de Software, pp. 13–25 (2017)
5. McKee, K.K., Forbes, G.L., Mazhar, I., Entwistle, R., Howard, I.: A review of machinery diagnostics and prognostics implemented on a centrifugal pump. In: Lee, J., Ni, J., Sarangapani, J., Mathew, J. (eds.) Engineering Asset Management 2011. LNME, pp. 593–614. Springer, London (2014). https://doi.org/10.1007/978-1-4471-4993-4_52
6. Cabral, I., Borges, N., Santolin, R.: Proposta de implementação da lógica e conceito de sistema andon no processo produtivo de estruturas metálicas. In: Encontro Nacional de Engenharia de Producao, no. 36, pp. 1–15 (2016)
7. Toasa, R., Silva, C., Silva, C., Goncalves, D., Neves, L., Marcelino, L.: Energy consumption behaviour characterization with mobile gamification. In: Iberian Conference on Information Systems and Technologies, CISTI, no. 7975900 (2017)
8. Silva, C., Toasa, R., Martinez, H., Veloz, J., Gallardo, C.: Secure push notification service based on MQTT protocol for mobile platforms. In: XII Jornadas Iberoamericanas de Ingeniería de Software e Ingeniería del Conocimiento y Congreso Ecuatoriano en Ingeniería de Software, pp. 69–84 (2017)
9. Nedyalkova, S.: Mobile web applications. Ph.D. thesis. Instituto Politécnico de Coimbra, Coimbra (2013)
10. Ahmed, R., Ramanathan, P., Saluja, K.: Necessary and sufficient conditions for thermal schedulability of periodic real-time tasks. In: Euromicro Conference on Real-Time Systems, pp. 243–525 (2014)
11. Xu, Y., et al.: Scheduling tasks with mixed timing constraints. In: ACM International Conference on Supercomputing (ICS), pp. 30 –43 (2016)
12. Pazmiño, R.: Sistema informático para control y monitoreo basado en el sistema de control andon para mejorar el desempeño de procesos y control de recursos en la manufactura de calzado de cuero. Faculty of Engineering Systems, Electronics and Industrial, Universidad Técnica de Ambato, Ambato (2017)
13. Yinglian, L., Bøegh, J., Qi, S.: Who can haul the ANDON-CORD in the software development process. In: Yuan, Y., Wu, X., Lu, Y. (eds.) ISCTCS 2012. CCIS, vol. 320, pp. 714–720. Springer, Heidelberg (2013). https://doi.org/10.1007/978-3-642-35795-4_90
14. Suárez, A., Jorge, F.: Análisis de los efectos de la implementación de un sistema andon en una planta ensambladora de vehiculos para el aumento de la productividad: caso aymesa sa. Master's thesis, PUCE (2015)
15. Lei, G., Lu, G., Sang, Y.: Design of wireless Andon system based on zigbee. In: Biomedical Engineering and Informatics (BMEI), pp. 821–825 (2015)
16. Jacobs, R., Chanse, R.: Administración De Operaciones. Producción Y Cadena De Suministros. Mc Graw-Hill/Interamericana Editores S.A., Mexico, Disttrito Federal (2014)

17. Yongzhen, L., Jing, L.: The research on ARP protocol based authentication mechanism. In: International Conference on Applied Mathematics, Simulation and Modelling, vol. 3, no. 78 (2016)
18. PostgreSQL: Postgresql portal en español (2016). http://www.postgresql.org.es
19. Elhorst, P.: Matlab software for spatial panels. Int. Reg. Sci. Rev. **37**, 389–405 (2014)

GPS Trajectory Compression Algorithm

Gary Reyes Zambrano$^{(\boxtimes)}$

Ecuador Facultad de Ciencias Matemáticas y Físicas, University of Guayaquil,
Cdla. Salvador Allende, Av. Delta y Av. Kennedy, Casilla Postal 471,
Guayaquil, Ecuador
gary.reyesz@ug.edu.ec

Abstract. This research is oriented toward the development of a trajectory compression algorithm for global positioning systems. In order to increase the compression ratio of the data, an algorithm is developed based on the algorithm of compression of GPS trajectories Top Down - Time Ratio. The algorithm is composed of a filter for noise reduction and makes use of semantic information to accept or discard relevant points of the trajectory. The experiments of the algorithm were carried out using three trajectory datasets: Mobile Century Data, Geolife Trajectories and T-Drive Data, increasing the compression ratio of the data, which leads to improvements in efficiency. With the results obtained, statistical tests were performed that allowed us to compare the results, compare it with other trajectory compression algorithms and validate the investigation.

Keywords: Compression · GPS data analysis · GPS data simplification

1 Introduction

Data compression process consists on taking a sequence of symbols and transforming them into codes, if the compression is effective, the resulting sequence of codes will be smaller than the original symbols [1]. This process should preserve the statistical purposes and other characteristics of the data while reducing the size [2]. The preservation of data properties and reduction levels depends on the compression algorithm used.

Compression algorithms can be classified into two categories, lossless compression algorithms and lossy compression algorithms. Lossless compression algorithms perform a more accurate reconstruction of the original data without loss of information. In contrast, lossy compression algorithms are inaccurate compared to the original data [3].

A GPS trajectory is represented as a discrete sequence of geographic coordinate points [4]. There are currently active research areas related to GPS trajectories. Among them is the GPS trajectory preprocessing area which studies the techniques and algorithms of trajectory compression. This algorithm remove some sub-traces of the original trajectory [5]; reducing data storage space and data transfer time.

Reducing the data size of a GPS trajectory makes it easier to speed up the information extraction process [6]. There are several methods of trajectory compression that are suitable for different types of data and produce different results, but they all have the same principle in common: compress the data by eliminating redundancy of the data in the source file [7–9].

© Springer Nature Switzerland AG 2019
M. Botto-Tobar et al. (Eds.): ICCCE 2018, CCIS 959, pp. 57–69, 2019.
https://doi.org/10.1007/978-3-030-12018-4_5

The bibliography describes a set of algorithms for the compression or simplification of GPS trajectories and their limitations [10–13] among which are highlighted:

- Douglas-Peucker: Does not compress data in real time.
- Visvalingam: The error rate and processing time are high.
- TD-TR: The error rate of the algorithm is high and does not compress data in real time.
- Opening Window: Its main disadvantage is the frequent removal or distortion of important points such as sharp angles. A secondary limitation is that straight lines are still overrepresented. For its correct functioning requires high hardware performance.
- ST-Trace: The processing time is considerable and requires speed information to characterize the trace.
- None of the algorithms consider the noise present in the trajectory data, which reduces the possibility of eliminating noisy points and improving the process of simplifying points.
- Only Squish and Dots algorithms perform a rigorous analysis of the GPS trajectory decoding procedure, but do not consider the analysis of trajectory noise.
- Douglas Peucker, Visvalingam and Opening Window algorithms only perform spatial analysis of the data. This eliminate temporary information that provides important data for better compression rates.
- The Visvalingam compression algorithm eliminates or distorts points, such as sharp angles, so the resulting trajectory may lack of important points to reconstruct a route.
- None of the algorithms consider the semantic information of the trajectory, wasting the opportunity to make an analysis that allows to discard more points of little meaning from the original trajectory.

This article describes an enhanced algorithm for GPS trajectory compression. In the previous works section, an analysis of the GPS trajectory compression algorithms is done. The GPS trajectory compression algorithm section describes the algorithm developed in this research. In the analysis of the results section the results obtained are shown. In the section on conclusions and future work, the main conclusion and the future work is presented.

2 Background Work

In this section, the algorithms described in the literature are analyzed in order to determine the main elements involved in the compression of GPS trajectory data. As part of the analysis, a review of different behaviors and conditions affecting GPS trajectory compression was conducted using various algorithms proposed in the literature. Table 1 shows the results of previous review.

Table 1. Behavior and conditions that affect GPS trajectory compression

Article	Year	Compression behavior	Conditions affecting the compression ratio
A new perspective on trajectory compression techniques	2003	Improved compression ratio by measuring error distances between synchronized positions	Type of trip (unidirectional, multidirectional), type of transport (taxi, bus)
Compressing trajectories using inter-frame coding	2010	The experimental compression ratio with uninterrupted trajectories is similar to the theoretical compression ratio	Short trajectories, uninterrupted trajectories
A trajectory compression algorithm based on non-uniform quantization	2015	Improves compression rate when processing data from large-scale trajectories in a geographic context	Geographical context (road networks or routes), cars, planes, ships
Improvement of OPW-TR algorithm for compressing GPS trajectory data	2017	Improves compression rate while decreasing data loss	The shape of the trajectory does not consider temporal information

2.1   Line Compression Algorithm

This algorithm, also known as line generalization or Lang's algorithm [14–16], works on the basis of the analysis of three points at the same time. The first three points are chosen and a line is drawn between the first and third points. If the distance between the line and the second point is greater than the defined tolerance, the second point is selected to analyze from the second point to the fourth point. If the distance is smaller than the tolerance, the second point is eliminated and the process is repeated from the third point to the fifth point and so on with the rest of the coordinates.

For the calculation of the given straight line, the formula 1 is used:

$$(x - x_1)/(x_2 - x_1) = (y - y_1)/(y_2 - y_1) \tag{1}$$

For the calculation of the distance between a line and a point the formula 2 is used:

$$|A * xp + B * yp + C|A2 + B^2 \tag{2}$$

2.2   Douglas-Peucker GPS Trajectory Compression Algorithm

Douglas-Peucker (DP) is a GPS trajectory compression algorithm based on the top-down method for data analysis. It is used to remove a series of line segments from a curve, which reduces the amount of data present in a GPS trajectory [17]. It's a line generalization algorithm. Recursively select points from the original series of GPS trajectory points [18–21].

Douglas-Peucker implements a divide and conquer strategy and is computed in four steps [22, 23]:

– The first and last node of a polygonal string are taken as the end points of a line.
– For all intermediate points, the shortest distance to this line is determined. If it is greater than any distance, the polygonal chain is separated by the point with the greatest distance, forming two new segments.
– The new segments formed are analyzed using the same procedure.
– The algorithm ends when it does not exceed any point line distance.

The computational complexity of the algorithm in the worst case is $O(n^2)$, where n is the number of original points. The computational complexity of the algorithm in the worst case can be improved to $O(n \log_n)$ using an approach involving convex hulls [6].

2.3   Top Down Time Ratio Line Simplification Algorithm

This algorithm is a modification of the Douglas-Peucker algorithm where the time variable is added. To do this, the coordinates of the point P_i' in time are calculated using the ratio of two time intervals.

$$\Delta_e = t_e - t_s \tag{3}$$

The difference between the time of the point to be analyzed and the time of the starting point is calculated using the formula 4:

$$\Delta_i = t_i - t_s \tag{4}$$

To obtain the coordinates of P_i', formulas 5 and 6 are applied:

$$x_i' = x_s + \frac{\Delta_i}{\Delta_e}(x_e - x_s) \tag{5}$$

$$y_i' = y_s + \frac{\Delta_i}{\Delta_e}(y_e - y_s) \tag{6}$$

After obtaining the coordinates, the synchronous Euclidean distance between P_i' and P_i, is calculated. If the distance is greater than the tolerance, this reference point is taken and the calculation of the intervals is performed again. The computational complexity in the worst case is $O(n^2)$. $O(n \log_n)$ implementation enhancement for Douglas-Peucker that takes advantage of geometric properties cannot be applied to TD-TR [24].

2.4   Visvalingam-Whyatt Algorithm

The Visvalingam-Whyatt algorithm use the concept of effective area, which is defined as the area of the triangle formed by a point and its two neighbors. The algorithm takes a poly-line P as the sequence of points, and the spatial displacement error is defined by the user. For each set of three consecutive points a triangle is formed, this being the effective area. Iteratively, the point that produces the least displacement of the area is selected to form an approximation. This process stops when the effective area is larger than ε [10, 21].

2.5 Experimental Analysis of the Algorithms

As part of the research process, an experiment was conducted with the analyzed algorithms. The results can be seen in Table 2.

Table 2. Comparative table of the analyzed algorithms

Algorithms	Execution time (seg)	Compression ratio (%)	Error rate
Douglas-Peucker	50,06	19,00	0,0225
Line simplification algorithm	154,69	99,49	0,0491
Visvalingam	280,99	32,84	0,0333
TD-TR	1512,57	99,60	0,0391

The experiment consists of running all the algorithms using the same database. The table shows the results obtained, from which it is decided to use the TD-TR line simplification algorithm as base for the selection of points in the compression algorithm proposed in this research.

3 GPS Trajectory Compression Algorithm

In this research, a GPS trajectory compression algorithm called GR-B is proposed. The algorithm consists in three stages.

1. Noise reduction
2. Line simplification

   • Simplification of semantic points
   • Point simplification based on TD-TR

3. Data compression

The algorithm has as input the GPS trajectory dataset to be compressed and as output the compressed GPS trajectory dataset. It starts with the application of an algorithm based on the noise reduction logic of the Kalman algorithm to eliminate all points that are considered noise. The output of this step is the input for the point simplification logic used in the TD-TR algorithm, in which the spatial and temporal elements of the data are taken into account. To improve the simplification of points in the TD-TR algorithm, semantic analysis of the trajectory is used.

Once the data has been simplified, compression is carried out using the Brotli algorithm. The data is divided into three independent vectors to compress each vector, resulting in three smaller compressed files. As a result of applying these three steps you have a set of compressed GPS data.

3.1   Noise Reduction Using Kalman's Algorithm Logic

This algorithm initially builds a model, closely related to the trajectory to be analyzed, in order to adjust the filter.

Functions 7 and 8 are used to build the model:

$$X_k = Ax_{k-1} + Bu_k + W_{k-1} \tag{7}$$

$$Z_k = Hx_k + V_k \tag{8}$$

The process values are then initialized based on the values of the first latitude and longitude point of the GPS trajectory. The values are initialized using prediction (9 and 10) and correction (11, 12 and 13) functions [25].

Functions for time update (Prediction):

$$X_k = Ax_{k-1} + Bu_k \tag{9}$$

$$P_k = AP_{k-1}A^t + Q \tag{10}$$

Measurement update functions (Correction):

$$K_k = P_k H^t \left(HP_k H^T + R \right)^{-1} \tag{11}$$

$$X_k = X_k + K_k(z_k - Hx_k) \tag{12}$$

$$P_k = (1 - K_k H)P_k \tag{13}$$

Once all the necessary information has been collected and the values have been initialized, the estimations can be repeated. Each point estimation is based on the previous point entry. The iterative process of the Kalman filter is decomposed in two stages: (1) the prediction of the state from the previous state is observed in the formula 9 and 10 and (2) the correction of the prediction using the observation of the current state is observed in the formulas 11, 12 and 13.

3.2   Trajectory Point Simplification

The simplification stage starts with the drawing of the initial line segment between the first and last points. Then, using the synchronous Euclidean distance, the distances from all points to the line segment are calculated, the point furthest from the line segment (or the maximum distance) is identified and marked. If the distance from the selected point to the line segment is less than the defined tolerance, all unmarked points are discarded, otherwise select the marked point for evaluation with the semantic layer and continue to divide the linear segment with this point. This procedure is executed recursively.

If the point is marked, then it is evaluated with the semantic layer to decide whether or not it can be added to the final simplified trajectory. To evaluate a marked point, the distance from the maximum circle of the point to all semantic points is calculated using the function 14

$$\cos(d) = (\sin a \, \sin b) + (\cos a \, \cos b \cos |c|) \tag{14}$$

Where a and b represent latitudes in degrees and c represents the absolute value of the longitude difference between the respective coordinates. A point is accepted if the distance to the nearest semantic point is less than the semantic tolerance.

3.3 Lossless Compression

For the compression of the resulting points, the lossless compression algorithm Botli [26–28] was selected and applied as stated in the literature. The application of this algorithm makes it possible the reduction of the space needed to store the GPS trajectories. This stage is a second line of data compression by which no data is lost.

Brotli is a compression algorithm announced by Google in September 2015. Brotli's decompression is as fast as gzip while significantly improving the compression ratio. The disadvantage is that compression is slower than gzip. This algorithm compresses the data using a sequence of bytes, starting with the first byte on the right side and proceeding to the left, with the most significant bit of each byte on the left. In this way, the result can be analyzed from right to left, with elements of fixed width in the correct order of msb-to-lsb and prefix codes in bit-reversed.

A compressed dataset consists on a header and a series of meta blocks. Each meta block decompresses to a sequence of 0 to 16,777,216 (16 MB) uncompressed bytes. The uncompressed final data is the concatenation of the uncompressed sequences of each meta block. The header contains the size of the slider window that was used during compression. The decompressor must retain at least the same amount of uncompressed data before the current position in the stream in order to decompress what follows. The size of the slider window is a power of two, minus 16, where the power is in the range of 10 to 24.

Each meta block is compressed using a combination of the LZ77 algorithm and Huffman coding. The result of Huffman's coding is called a "prefix code". The prefix codes for each meta block are independent of the previous or subsequent meta blocks. The LZ77 algorithm can use a reference to a duplicate string that occurs in a previous meta block, up to the size of a sliding window of uncompressed bytes before.

The meta block consists of two parts: a header describing the representation of the compressed data and the compressed data. Compressed data consists on a series of commands. Each command consists of two parts: a sequence of literal bytes (of strings that have not been detected as duplicates within the slider window) and a pointer to a duplicate string, which is represented as a <length, backward distance> pair. There can be zero literal bytes in the command. The minimum length of the string to duplicate is two, but the last command in the meta block is allowed to have only literal and no pointer to a string to duplicate.

4 Analysis of the Results

Three experiments are conducted to evaluate the results of the GR-B algorithm. The first experiment is designed to measure the amount of disk space occupied by the data compressed with the proposed algorithm. The second experiment is designed to validate the compression ratio and the error rate of the TD-TR algorithm and the algorithm developed until the simplification stage. The third experiment is designed to evaluate the compression ratio of the developed algorithm compared to other algorithms proposed in the literature. In the first experiment a random trajectory called the X trajectory is selected and the GR-B algorithm is applied to compress the GPS trajectory points. The result of the experiment is the number of points, the disk space occupied by the compressed trajectory and the compression rate. The original X trajectory is formed by a total of 7591 vehicle GPS trajectory points and takes up 776 kb of disk space initially. After applying the GR-B algorithm the number of end points of the trajectory is 11, occupying 1.18 kb of disk space with a compression rate of 99.86%. After the experiment it was possible to verify that it is possible to reconstruct the trajectory using only the points resulting from the compression process.

The second experiment is designed to evaluate the compression ratio and the error rate. For this purpose, the TD-TR algorithm and the developed algorithm until the simplification stage are executed. This experiment is intended to check whether the parameters are significantly improved with respect to the TD-TR algorithm. It is defined as a null hypothesis (Ho) for experiment 1 that 'sample groups conform to a normal distribution'. Seven observations from the California database were selected for the execution of the experiment with the following characteristics:

- Observation 1: Forty-five trajectories, each one containing between 550 and 1200 points.
- Observation 2: Forty-two trajectories, each one containing between 650 and 1200 points.
- Observation 3: Forty-two trajectories, each one containing between 750 and 1200 points.
- Observation 4: Forty-two trajectories, each one containing between 1000 and 3000 points.
- Observation 5: Two hundred and forty-four trajectories, each one containing between 2000 and 4000 points.
- Observation 6: Forty-two trajectories, each one containing between 2000 and 4000 points.
- Observation 7: Thirty-nine trajectories, each one containing between 4000 and 9000 points.

Table 3 shows the results obtained from the experiments, which are statistically processed using Shapiro-Wilk's test to check the assumption of normality of the data. Figure 1 shows that the values are not adjusted to a normal distribution with a p-value equals to 0.0001402 and 0.3645. Therefore, the null hypothesis (Ho) for the metric, error margin, is rejected and in the metric compression ratio, Fig. 2 shows that the

Table 3. Test results

Tests	Number of points	Number of trajectories	Assumption of normality (compression ratio)	Assumption of normality (margin of error)	Assumption of normality (compression ratio)	Assumption of normality (margin of error)
1	550–1200	45	Rejected Ho	Not rejected Ho	Rejected Ho	Not rejected Ho
2	650–1200	42	Rejected Ho	Not rejected Ho	Rejected Ho	Not rejected Ho
3	750–1200	42	Rejected Ho	Not rejected Ho	Rejected Ho	Not rejected Ho
4	1000–3000	42	Rejected Ho	Not rejected Ho	Rejected Ho	Not rejected Ho
5	2000	244	Rejected Ho	Not rejected Ho	Rejected Ho	Not rejected Ho
6	2000–4000	42	Rejected Ho	Not rejected Ho	Rejected Ho	Not rejected Ho
7	4000–9000	39	Rejected Ho	Not rejected Ho	Rejected Ho	Not rejected Ho

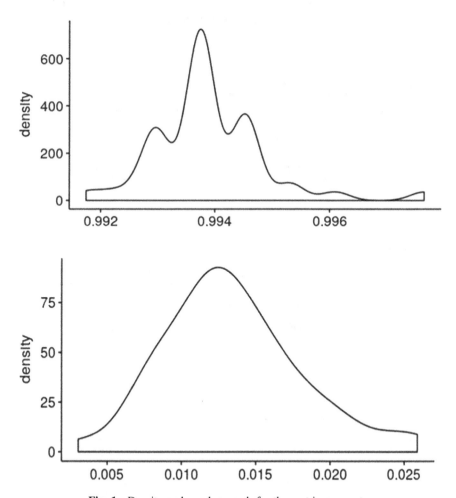

Fig. 1. Density and p-value graph for the metric error rate.

values of the sample are adjusted to a normal distribution with p-values equals to 001621, 0.0003759 and 0.0003857, therefore, the null hypothesis (Ho) is not rejected.

Subsequently, the Mann-Whitney test is applied, obtaining p-values lower than 0.05, which shows significant differences according to the test applied with 95% of confidence. Finally, the Fischer test is applied to check the assumption of the homogeneity of the variances and the Student test to compare the means of the results obtained for the metric error rate. In the application of the Fisher test, it is observed that the p-values obtained are greater than 0.05, so the homogeneity mentioned above is assumed. Once the assumption of homogeneity has been verified, the Student test is applied to compare the vector means of the results obtained for the metric error rate. From the analysis of the p-values obtained, greater than 0.05, it can be concluded that the means of the compared groups are significantly similar. All tests were performed with 95% confidence. The verification performed can ensure that the compression ratio of the proposed algorithm using only the first two steps is better than TD-TR simplification algorithm. It is evident that the error rate remains the same.

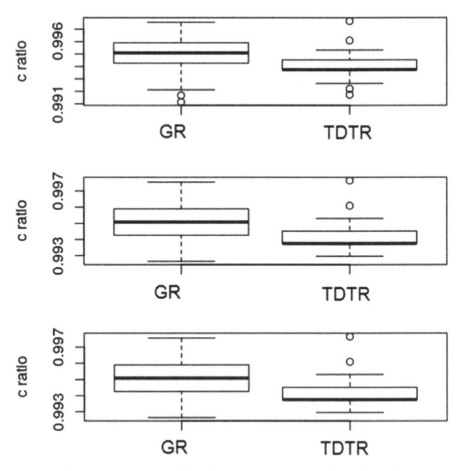

Fig. 2. P-value chart and box diagrams for the compression ratio metric

As third experiment, the evaluation of the compression ratio of the algorithm developed with statistical tests is proposed. The performance of the lossless compression algorithms Brotli, bzip2, gzip, xz is compared with the algorithm developed up to the simplification stage. This experiment is designed to determine which lossless compression algorithm is best suited to the solution. Four observations with the following characteristics are selected:

- Observation 1: three hundred trajectories, each one containing between 300 and 2500 points.
- Observation 2: three hundred trajectories, each containing between 310 and 4000 points.
- Observation 3: three hundred trajectories, each one containing between 320 and 2000 points.
- Observation 4: three hundred trajectories, each one containing between 360 and 2000 points.

The p-values obtained by the compression ratio metric to check the assumption of normality is $2.2e{-}16$. This evidence that they do not fit a normal distribution therefore Ho is rejected. The Kruscal-Wallis test is then applied to compare several independent groups that do not fit to a normal distribution. The p-values obtained are less than 0.05, which means that there are significant differences according to the test applied with 95% of confidence. The median values obtained are higher for the GR-B algorithm so it can be concluded that has the best compression ratio.

5   Conclusions and Future Work

The study of noise reduction, line simplification and semantics in GPS trajectory compression allowed the foundation of a GPS trajectory compression algorithm that improves the compression ratio compared to those present in the literature. The comparison of the main algorithms for GPS trajectory compression demonstrated that TD-TR has the highest compression ratio in the experimental data set used and is therefore used as the basis for the simplification of points in the developed algorithm. The aim of the research is to increase the compression ratio while maintaining the margin of error, which is demonstrated by the results obtained from the processed data. These results are validated by means of statistical tests. The performed experiments show that the proposed GPS trajectory compression algorithm shows a greater compression ratio compared to similar ones analyzed in the literature, which reduces the amount of data to be processed. As you can see, the proposed algorithm compresses the GPS trajectory data in a significant way. As future work, it is planned to perform these experiments on other types of trajectories with a lower level of data redundancy and make the necessary adjustments to the algorithm to maintain the results achieved.

References

1. Chen, M., Xu, M., Fränti, P.: A fast O(N) multi-resolution polygonal approximation algorithm for GPS trajectory simplification. IEEE Trans. Image Process. 1–14 (2012)
2. Wang, T.: An online data compression algorithm for trajectories. Int. J. Inf. Educ. Technol. **3** (4), 480–487 (2013)
3. Stacchini, J.C., Lessa, T., Pal, B.: Data compression in smart distribution systems via singular value decomposition. IEEE Trans. Smart Grid **8**(1), 275–284 (2017)
4. Corcoran, P., Mooney, P., Huang, G.: Unsupervised trajectory compression. In: IEEE International Conference on Robotics and Automation (ICRA), pp. 3126–3132 (2016)
5. Ji, Y., Liu, H., Liu, X., Ding, Y., Luo, W.: A comparison of road-network-constrained trajectory compression methods. In: IEEE 22nd International Conference on Parallel and Distributed Systems (2016)
6. Muckell, J., Olsen, P.W., Lawson, C., Ravi, S., Hwang, J.: Compression of trajectory data: a comprehensive evaluation and new approach. Geoinformatica **2014**, 435–460 (2014)
7. Salomon, D.: Data Compression, 4th edn. Springer, London (2007). https://doi.org/10.1007/978-1-84628-603-2
8. Gudmundsson, J., Katajainen, J., Merrick, D., Ong, C., Wolle, T.: Compressing spatio-temporal trajectories. Comput. Geom. Theory Appl. **42**(9), 825–841 (2009)
9. Lv, C., Chen, F., Xu, Y., Song, J., Lv, P.: A trajectory compression algorithm based on non-uniform quantization. In: 12th International Conference on Fuzzy Systems and Knowledge Discovery (FSKD), pp. 2469–2474 (2015)
10. Van Hunnik, R.: Extensive comparison of trajectory simplification algorithms. University Utrecht (2017)
11. Asif, M.T., Kannan, S., Dauwels, J., Jaillet, P.: Data compression techniques for urban traffic data. In: 2013 IEEE Symposium on Computational Intelligence in Vehicles and Transportation Systems (CIVTS), pp. 4–9 (2013)
12. Meratnia, N., de By, R.A.: Spatiotemporal compression techniques for moving point objects. In: Bertino, E., Christodoulakis, S., Plexousakis, D., Christophides, V., Koubarakis, M., Böhm, K., Ferrari, E. (eds.) EDBT 2004. LNCS, vol. 2992, pp. 765–782. Springer, Heidelberg (2004). https://doi.org/10.1007/978-3-540-24741-8_44
13. Lawson, C., Ravi, S., Hwang, J.-H.: Compression and mining of GPS trace data: new techniques and applications, New York (2011)
14. Zhilin, L.: An algorithm for compressing digital contour data. Cartogr. J. **25**, 143–146 (1998)
15. Rhind, D.W.: Generalisation and realism within automated cartographic systems. Can. Cartogr. **10**(1), 51–62 (1973)
16. McMaster, R., Shea, K.S.: Generalization in Digital Cartography. Association of American Geographers, Washington, D.C. (1992)
17. Sim, M., Kwak, J.-H., Lee, C.-H.: Fast shape matching algorithm based on the improved Douglas-Peucker algorithm. KIPS Trans. Softw. Data Eng. **5**(10), 497–502 (2016)
18. Wu, S., Silva, A.C.G., Márquez, M.R.G.: The Douglas-Peucker algorithm: sufficiency conditions for non-self-intersections. J. Brazilian Comput. Soc. **9**, 1–17 (2004)
19. Lin, X., Ma, S., Zhang, H., Wo, T., Huai, J.: One-pass error bounded trajectory simplification. In: 43rd International Conference on Very Large Data Bases (VLDB), pp. 841–852 (2017)
20. Wang, H.: SharkDB : an in-memory storage system for large scale trajectory data management. The University of Queensland (2016)
21. Visvalingam, M., Whyatt, J.D.: Line generalisation by repeated elimination of the smallest area. Cartographic Information Systems Research Group, July 1992

22. Koegel, M., Mauve, M., Baselt, D., Scheuermann, B.: A comparison of vehicular trajectory encoding techniques. In: The 10th IFIP Annual Mediterranean Ad Hoc Networking Workshop, pp. 87–94 (2011)
23. Zhang, S., Liu, Z., Cai, Y., Wu, Z., Shi, G.: AIS trajectories simplification and threshold determination. J. Navig. **2016**, 729–744 (2016)
24. Hershberger, J., Snoeyink, J.: Speeding up the Douglas-Peucker line-simplification algorithm (1992)
25. Bianco, J.: Estudio y aplicación de Filtros de Kalman sobre sistemas de posicionamiento global para el suavizado de trayectorias geoposicionadas. Universidad Nacional de Córdoba (2013)
26. Cegan, L.: Empirical study on effects of compression algorithms in web environment. J. Telecommun. Electron. Comput. Eng. **9**(2), 69–72 (2017)
27. Alakuijala, J., Kliuchnikov, E., Szabadka, Z., Vandevenne, L.: Comparison of Brotli, Deflate, Zopfli, LZMA, LZHAM and Bzip2 compression algorithms (2015)
28. Matejek, B., Haehn, D., Lekschas, F., Mitzenmacher, M., Pfister, H.: Compresso: efficient compression of segmentation data for connectomics. In: Descoteaux, M., Maier-Hein, L., Franz, A., Jannin, P., Collins, D.L., Duchesne, S. (eds.) MICCAI 2017. LNCS, vol. 10433, pp. 781–788. Springer, Cham (2017). https://doi.org/10.1007/978-3-319-66182-7_89

Computer and Software Engineering

Algebraic Model to Formalize the Sentences and Their Context for Texts Written in the Spanish Language

Edgardo Samuel Barraza Verdesoto[1(✉)], Edwin Rivas Trujillo[2(✉)], and Víctor Hugo Medina García[2(✉)]

[1] University of Seville, Seville, Spain
edgbarver@alum.us.es
[2] University Distrital Francisco José de Caldas, Bogotá, Colombia
erivas@udistrital.edu.co, victorhmedina@gmail.com

Abstract. This paper introduces a model based on set theory and modern algebra that formalizes sentences and their context. The model aims at dividing sentences into cores which will be mapped into sets of an algebraic space; some of these cores have a type of context called *strictly linguistic context*. These sets along with an operation form *Abelian groups*. In addition, the model defines a function that can completely (or partially) restore the original sentence from such sets while guaranteeing its structure and meaning. This could be accomplished through queries that compare contexts and activate the task of restoring sentences. The use case scenario has been limited to the Spanish language. All these processes can be applied in many scenarios, but our focus lies in the dynamic creation of small theories.

Keywords: Algebraic structure · Abelian group · Context · Nominal phrases · Verbal cores · Small theories

1 Introduction

The study of the *context*, its formalization and its influence on language production, decision making, automatic reasoning, and other fields, has been analyzed by many disciplines: pragmatics [1], neuroscience [2–4], psycholinguistics [5], and computer science [6–12]. Their works has given birth to models which answer questions such as "what is the context?" or "how to use it?", sometimes from different points of view. The purpose of this article consists on modeling a sentence and one type of context known as *strictly linguistic context* [13,14] which is contained inside of the sentences and provides the necessary environment to understand the message.

Building ontologies [15] for large amounts of data is a task that can involve applications such as *Text2Onto* [16] or *OntoLearn* [17] which can convert texts

© Springer Nature Switzerland AG 2019
M. Botto-Tobar et al. (Eds.): ICCCE 2018, CCIS 959, pp. 73–86, 2019.
https://doi.org/10.1007/978-3-030-12018-4_6

into ontologies. *Microtheories* [8] represent an alternative solution; they are small theories that can coexist with contradicting theories [18] because they require a different *context* to complete their own semantics. The common approach involves building theories based on an entire text and storing them in a monolithic knowledge base. The novelty of the proposed solution lies in organizing a text by modules that can be chosen, manipulated or matched conveniently, and without losing of its meaning, through operations created within the context of algebraic structures. Hence, ontologies, theories or small theories could be dynamically built from portions of the text or by associating parts taken from several texts. This paper introduces some objects that can drive the dynamic creation of small theories. One of these objects, called a *nominal core*, is an expression without verbs, that still has a meaning; they are embedded within the sentences and contain *strictly linguistic context*. The *nominal cores* could be a starting point to compare topics or to establish relationships within the same sentence, between two or more sentences, or even with other texts. Although the study of these elements remains a part of the research, this paper will only present a *formalization of the sentences and their context based on such cores*.

The document is organized as follow, the first section introduces the model by explaining its components and roles, the second section analyzes a heuristic-based system for the Spanish language that is capable of dissociating texts into *verbal and nominal cores* to fill the sets of the model. The third section shows the results from the dissociating experiment carried out. Finally, conclusions are drawn on the overall work and future work is also discussed.

2   The Model

In this section, the basics concepts of the algebraic model are defined as well as some axioms and theorems required to formalize the model. The use case scenario in this model only includes the sentences in the Spanish language. Therefore, some concepts and processes are aimed at that specific context[1].

2.1   The Context of a Sentence

The context involved in the sentences belongs to an explicit category and it is called a *strictly linguistic context* [13,14] which is the set of all factors that accompany a word by affecting its interpretation, its consistency, and its meaning [19]. *Nominal phrases* are *sequences of words* that contain this type of context [20,21].

2.2   Sets and Processes

A general overview of the model is shown in Fig. 1. The system's dynamics starts with a process called *dissociation* that divides a sentence into linguistic

---

[1] We would like to express our appreciation to Duvań Cardona Sańchez for his support in the mathematical area.

categories using a parser [22]. Subsequently, a set of *heuristics* reprocesses the parser's output leading to two types of clusters: *nominal cores* and *verbal cores*. These will be defined latter.

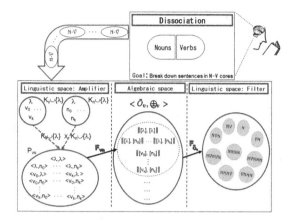

Fig. 1. Processes and sets of the model

Each time that a *nominal core* or a *verbal core* is generated, it is then inserted into a set called K_n or K_v respectively. As soon as the sentence has been completely processed, the *Cartesian Product* $K_v \bigcup \{\lambda\} \times K_n \bigcup \{\lambda\}$ takes place, and new elements are added to P_{vn}. These processes are repeated for each sentence contained in the text. Table 1 illustrates the result obtained on the sentence: *"Toda clase de establecimientos comerciales podremos encontrar en las calles Velásquez y Tetúan"*. For this implementation, all sentences are expected with a verb starting the expression, and the verb v_0 is missing. Formally, the sets and their elements are defined as follows:

Table 1. Cores and Cartesian product of a sentence

Word	Category
Toda, clase, de, establecimientos, comerciales	n_0: nominal-core (pron, n, p, n, adj)
podremos, encontrar	v_1: verbal-core (v, v)
en, las, calles, Velásquez, y, Tetúan	n_1: nominal-core (p, a, n, N, c, N)
Cartesian product	
$<\lambda, \lambda>, <\lambda, n_0>, <\lambda, n_1>$	$<v_1, \lambda>, <v_1, n_0>, <v_1, n_1>$

Axiom 1. The empty (null) sequence of words *exists and it is denoted as λ*.

Definition 1 (The set K_n). *Let us denote K_n as the set that contains **nominal cores**. In this model, a cluster of words that contains a **nominal phrase** is known as a **nominal core**.*

Definition 2 (The set K_v). *Let us denote K_v as the set that contains **verbal cores** which are non-null **sequences of words** belonging to a sentence that has not nouns and at least one verb. They express an action, an existence, an achievement, or a state.*

Definition 3 (The set P_{vn}). *Let P_{vn} be the Cartesian product $K_v \bigcup \{\lambda\} \times K_n \bigcup \{\lambda\}$.*

2.3   The Algebraic Space

The set P_{vn} contains elements which are not good candidates for completely or partially representing the original sentence, e.g., the couple $<v_1, n_0>$ in Table 1 refers to: *podemos encontrar toda clase de establecimientos comerciales*, which does not correspond to any part of the original sentence and, what is worse is that the meaning could be altered. Hence, P_{vn} should be mapped to another *space* where the *cores* can be manipulated without loosing its consistency regarding to the original sentence. One set and one mapping are defined for this purpose.

Definition 4 (The set $\bar{O}_v$). *Let us denote $\bar{O}_v$ as the set containing couples of sequences in the form:*

$$\llbracket X \rrbracket = \llbracket [v_0 : v_1 : \cdots : v_k], [n_0 : n_1 : \cdots : n_k] \rrbracket$$

Each v_i belongs to $K_v \bigcup \{\lambda\}$, each n_i belongs to $K_n \bigcup \{\lambda\}$, and i is an index indicates the order in which the element was dissociated from the sentence. The following combinations are possible: $\llbracket [v], [n] \rrbracket$; $\llbracket [v], [\lambda] \rrbracket$; $\llbracket [\lambda], [n] \rrbracket$; or $\llbracket [\lambda], [\lambda] \rrbracket$.

The notation $\llbracket X_i \rrbracket$ is introduced to refer to a member of $\bar{O}_v$. Additionally, $\llbracket X_{a/b} \rrbracket$, where $a < b$, means that a member has λ elements before the subscript a and after the subscript b in both components; the notations $\llbracket [V_{a/b}], [N_{c/d}] \rrbracket$ or $\llbracket [v_{a/b}], [n_{c/d}] \rrbracket$ specify the same in each member component. Furthermore, the expression $\llbracket [v_i], [n_j] \rrbracket$ means that the couple has one member with a single element in each component, where each one has different positions.

*On the other hand, the notation $\lambda_{a/b}$ means that there are λ-**elements** between the positions **a** and **b**, with both included. If an element such as λ_k appears, this means that the λ-element exists in the kth position. A couple of sequences with only λ-elements can be modelled as $\llbracket [\lambda_{0/\infty}], [\lambda_{0/\infty}] \rrbracket$ that will be called Γ.*

Definition 5 (Function F_{vn}). *Let us define F_{vn} the injective function that maps a subset of pairs $<v_i, n_i> \in P_{vn}$ in pairs $\llbracket [v_i], [n_i] \rrbracket \in \bar{O}_v$.*

Figure 2 shows an implementation of the F_{vn} function applied to a sentence. The left box is a subset of P_{vn} and the right box corresponds to the mapping range related to $\bar{O}_v$; the superscript indicates the cardinality of the sets. The subsets of P_{vn} must comply with the following characteristics:

1. All members must contain **strictly linguistic context**. Hence, the set does not contain elements of the type $<v_i, \lambda>$, but elements such as $<\lambda, n_i>$ can be accepted.

2. Elements of the type $<v_i, n_j>$ must to have the same subscript $(i = j)$. The same subscript means that the *verbal core* is found immediately before of the *nominal core* inside of the sentence.

p_λ:$<\lambda, \lambda>$	P_{vn}^2: Subset of the Cartesian product	e_1:$[\lambda][\lambda]$	$\tilde{O}_v^7$: Mapping
p_0:$<\lambda, n_0$: La marcha$>$		e_0:$[\lambda][n_0]$	
p_1:$<\mathcal{V}_1$: *programada*, n_1:para el próximo 26 de marzo$>$		e_1:$[\lambda:\mathcal{V}_1][\lambda:n_1]$	
p_2:$<\mathcal{V}_2$:*que ha sido denominado*, n_2:día nacional$>$		e_2:$[\lambda:\lambda_1:\mathcal{V}_2][\lambda:\lambda:n_2]$	
p_3:$<\lambda, n_3$:por la vida$>$		e_3:$[\lambda:\lambda:\lambda:\lambda][\lambda:\lambda:\lambda:n_3]$	
p_4:$<\lambda, n_4$:,la Paz y la justicia$>$		e_4:$[\lambda:\lambda:\lambda:\lambda:\lambda][\lambda:\lambda:\lambda:\lambda:n_4]$	
p_5:$<\mathcal{V}_5$:,*recibía*, n_5:críticas$>$		e_5:$[\lambda:\lambda:\lambda:\lambda:\lambda:\mathcal{V}_5][\lambda:\lambda:\lambda:\lambda:\lambda:n_5]$	
p_6:$<\lambda, n_6$:ayer de parte de dos miembros del partido ARENA: Alfredo Cristiani y Jorge Velado$>$		e_6:$[\lambda:\lambda:\lambda:\lambda:\lambda:\lambda][\lambda:\lambda:\lambda:\lambda:\lambda:n_6]$	

Fig. 2. The figure shows the mapping of a sentence into the algebraic space

2.4   The Algebraic Structure

An algebraic structure composed by a set that has a *closure* property under an operation is introduced. The **closure** property is convenient since it allows the operation to generate new members in $\bar{O}_v$ without any connection to the subset of the P_{vn}.

Definition 6 (Operation $\oplus_v$). *In a natural manner, a binary operation $\oplus_v$ for couples belonging to $\bar{O}_v$ and its functionality are defined. The subscripts used are ordered as follows: $0 < i < j < k < m$.*

*Positionality and Duality. The binary operation $\oplus_v$ can be qualified as **dual** and **positional**. **Dual** means that if two members belonging to $\bar{O}_v$ are operated, then the operation occurs separately in the **verbal** and the **nominal** components. **Positional** means that two operands can be operated if and only if they have the same subscript. For example:*

$$[[\lambda_0 : v_1 : \lambda_2], [\lambda_0 : n_1 : \lambda_2]] \oplus_v [[\lambda_0 : \lambda_1 : v_2], [\lambda_0 : \lambda_1 : n_2]]$$
$$\Rightarrow [[\lambda_0 : v_1 : v_2], [\lambda_0 : n_1 : n_2]]$$

Gamma Cases. An operation between λ_i and x_i, with x_i characterizing a verbal core or a nominal core, will produce x_i. Hence, an operation between $[\![X_i]\!]$ and Γ occurs as follows:

$$[\![X_i]\!] \oplus_v \Gamma = \Gamma \oplus_v [\![X_i]\!] = [\![X_i]\!]$$

Null Cases. If two members of $\bar{O}_v$ having elements in their components with the same subscript are operated, the result of the operation in this position is λ. The following cases are possible:

1. $[\![X_{i/k}]\!] \oplus_v [\![X_{j/m}]\!] = [[v_{i/j-1} : \lambda_{j/k} : v_{k+1/m}], [n_{i/j-1} : \lambda_{j/k} : n_{k+1/m}]]$
2. $[\![X_{i/j}]\!] \oplus_v [\![X_{i/j}]\!] = [[\lambda_{0/j}], [\lambda_{0/j}]] = [[\lambda_{0/\infty}], [\lambda_{0/\infty}]] = \Gamma$

Abelian Group $<\bar{O}_v \oplus_v>$. The set $\bar{O}_v$ along with the binary operation $\oplus_v$ form an *Abelian Group structure* which is *finite* and *non-cyclic*. This means that the set for $\bar{O}_v$ is closed under the operation $\oplus_v$, that it is *associative*, that the *neutral and symmetrical elements* exist, and that it is *commutative*. The proof and the contribution of each property to the model are detailed.

Theorem 1 (Abelian Group $<\bar{O}_v \oplus_v>$).
    The set $\bar{O}_v$, along with the binary operation $\oplus_v$ forms an Abelian Group structure

Proof. It must be proven that the operation $\oplus_v$ is closed for $\bar{O}_v$, that it is associative, that the neutral and symmetrical elements exist, and that it is commutative. The subscripts used have the following order relation: $0 < i < k < m$

– Closure*: The* closure property *guarantees that an operation between two members of $\bar{O}_v$ always yields a member of $\bar{O}_v$. In this model, the operation generates new members in $\bar{O}_v$ by reducing or expanding the* context *in the couples. Formally, for all $[\![X_i]\!]$, $[\![X_j]\!]$ in $\bar{O}_v$, the result of the operation, $[\![X_i]\!] \oplus_v [\![X_j]\!]$, is also contained in $\bar{O}_v$.*
    Definition 6 shows all possibilities.

– Associative*: The* Associative property *states that the result of several operations executed sequentially is not affected by the order of their execution two-by-two execution, and, thus, their products will contain the same* context *and the same* meaning*. Formally, for all $[\![X_i]\!]$, $[\![X_j]\!]$ and $[\![X_k]\!]$ in $\bar{O}_v$, the equation $([\![X_i]\!] \oplus_v [\![X_j]\!]) \oplus_v [\![X_k]\!] = [\![X_i]\!] \oplus_v ([\![X_j]\!] \oplus_v [\![X_k]\!])$ holds. All possible cases are demonstrated as follows:*

1. $([\![[v_{i/k}],[n_{i/k}]]\!] \oplus_v [\![[v_{i/k}],[n_{i/k}]]\!]) \oplus_v [\![[v_{i/k}],[n_{i/k}]]\!] =$
$$[\![[v_{i/k}],[n_{i/k}]]\!] \oplus_v ([\![[v_{i/k}],[n_{i/k}]]\!] \oplus_v [\![[v_{i/k}],[n_{i/k}]]\!])$$
$\Gamma \oplus_v [\![[v_{i/k}],[n_{i/k}]]\!] = [\![[v_{i/k}],[n_{i/k}]]\!] \oplus_v \Gamma$
$[\![[v_{i/k}],[n_{i/k}]]\!] = [\![[v_{i/k}],[n_{i/k}]]\!]$

2. $([\![[v_{i/k}],[n_{i/k}]]\!] \oplus_v [\![[v_{i/k}],[n_{i/k}]]\!]) \oplus_v [\![[v_{i+1/k+1}],[n_{i+1/k+1}]]\!] =$
$$[\![[v_{i/k}],[n_{i/k}]]\!] \oplus_v ([\![[v_{i/k}],[n_{i/k}]]\!] \oplus_v [\![[v_{i+1/k+1}],[n_{i+1/k+1}]]\!])$$
$\Gamma \oplus_v [\![[v_{i+1/k+1}],[n_{i+1/k+1}]]\!] =$
$$[\![[v_{i/k}],[n_{i/k}]]\!] \oplus_v [\![[v_i : \lambda_{i+1/k} : v_{k+1}],[n_i : \lambda_{i+1/k} : n_{k+1}]]\!]$$
$[\![[v_{i+1/k+1}],[n_{i+1/k+1}]]\!] = [\![[v_{i+1/k+1}],[n_{i+1/k+1}]]\!]$

3. $([\![[v_{i/k}],[n_{i/k}]]\!] \oplus_v [\![[v_{i+1/k+1}],[n_{i+1/k+1}]]\!]) \oplus_v [\![[v_{i/k}],[n_{i/k}]]\!] =$
$$[\![[v_{i/k}],[n_{i/k}]]\!] \oplus_v ([\![[v_{i+1/k+1}],[n_{i+1/k+1}]]\!] \oplus_v [\![[v_{i/k}],[n_{i/k}]]\!])$$
$[\![[v_i : \lambda_{i+1/k} : v_{k+1}],[n_i : \lambda_{i+1/k} : n_{k+1}]]\!] \oplus_v [\![[v_{i/k}],[n_{i/k}]]\!] =$
$$[\![[v_{i/k}],[n_{i/k}]]\!] \oplus_v [\![[v_i : \lambda_{i+1/k} : v_{k+1}],[n_i : \lambda_{i+1/k} : n_{k+1}]]\!]$$
$[\![[v_{i+1/k+1}],[n_{i+1/k+1}]]\!] = [\![[v_{i+1/k+1}],[n_{i+1/k+1}]]\!]$

4. $([\![[v_{i/k}],[n_{i/k}]]\!] \oplus_v [\![[v_{i+1/k+1}],[n_{i+1/k+1}]]\!]) \oplus_v [\![[v_{i+1/k+1}],[n_{i+1/k+1}]]\!] =$
$$[\![[v_{i/k}],[n_{i/k}]]\!] \oplus_v ([\![[v_{i+1/k+1}],[n_{i+1/k+1}]]\!] \oplus_v [\![[v_{i+1/k+1}],[n_{i+1/k+1}]]\!])$$
$[\![[v_i : \lambda_{i+1/k} : v_{k+1}],[n_i : \lambda_{i+1/k} : n_{k+1}]]\!] \oplus_v [\![[v_{i+1/k+1}],[n_{i+1/k+1}]]\!] =$
$$[\![[v_{i/k}],[n_{i/k}]]\!]$$
$\oplus_v \Gamma$
$[\![[v_{i/k}],[n_{i/k}]]\!] = [\![[v_{i/k}],[n_{i/k}]]\!]$

5. $([[v_{i/k}],[n_{i/k}]] \oplus_v [[v_{k+1/j}],[n_{k+1/j}]]) \oplus_v [[v_{j+1/m}],[n_{j+1/m}]] =$

$\qquad [[v_{i/k}],[n_{i/k}]] \oplus_v ([[v_{k+1/j}],[n_{k+1/j}]] \oplus_v [[v_{j+1/m}],[n_{j+1/m}]])$

$[[v_{i/j}],[n_{i/j}]] \oplus_v [[v_{j+1/m}],[n_{j+1/m}]] =$

$\qquad\qquad\qquad\qquad [[v_{i/k}],[n_{i/k}]] \oplus_v [[v_{j/m}],[n_{j/m}]]$

$[[v_{i/m}],[n_{i/m}]] = [[v_{i/m}],[n_{i/m}]]$

- *Neutral and Symmetrical element:* Abelian groups *are endowed with a sym-metrical element providing richness to the operations, e.g., it is possible to delete or replace cores inside of the vectors due the* symmetrical element. *Fur-thermore, if the* neutral element *does not exist, neither does the* symmetrical element. *The* symmetrical element *of a member from* $<\bar{O}_v$ *is itself and the* neutral element *is* Γ.

  - Neutral element: *Suppose* $[X_i]$ *belongs to* $\bar{O}_v$. *There is an element* $[E]$ *such that:* $[X_i] \oplus_v [E] = [E] \oplus_v [X_i] = [X_i]$.
    By definition, the internal operation: $\Gamma \oplus_v [X_i] = [X_i] \oplus_v \Gamma = [X_i]$
    Thus, by uniqueness, $[E] = \Gamma$

  - Symmetrical element: $[X_i] \oplus_v [Y] = \Gamma$.
    If $[[v_{i/k}],[n_{i/k-1}]]$ *belongs to* $\bar{O}_v$, *then there exists an element* $[Y]$ *such that:*

$$[[v_{i/k}],[n_{i/k}]] \oplus_v [Y] = \Gamma$$

By definition of the operation, if there are two equal positional elements then the result is λ. *If all elements are equal one by one, then the resulting sequence is filled with* λ *which is equivalent to* Γ:

$$[[v_{i/k}],[n_{i/k}]] \oplus_v [[v_{i/k}],[n_{i/k}]] = [[\lambda_{i/k}],[\lambda_{i/k}]] = \Gamma$$

Thus, the symmetric element of any sequence exists and is equal to itself.

- Commutativity. *The commutativity property states that if two elements of the set* $\bar{O}_v$ *are operated, the final* context *and* meaning *will be the same. Suppose two elements* $[[v_{0/k}],[n_{0/k}]]$ *and* $[[v_{1/k+1}],[n_{1/k+1}]]$. *The* $\oplus_v$ *operation between them will be equal to:*
$[[v_0 : v_1 : \cdots : v_k : \lambda_{k+1}],[n_0 : n_1 : \cdots : n_k : \lambda_{k+1}]] \oplus_v$
$[[\lambda_0 : v_1 : \cdots : v_k : v_{k+1}],[\lambda_0 : n_1 : \cdots : n_k : n_{k+1}]]$

$[[v_0 : \lambda_1 : \cdots : \lambda_k : v_{k+1}],[n_0 : \lambda_1 : \cdots : \lambda_k : n_{k+1}]]$
$[[v_0 : \lambda_{1/k} : v_{k+1}],[n_0 : \lambda_{1/k} : n_{k+1}]]$ *(shortly)*

Now, if the operands are inverted, then:

$[[\lambda_0 : v_1 : \cdots : v_k : v_{k+1}],[\lambda_0 : n_1 : \cdots : n_k : n_{k+1}]] \oplus_v$
$[[v_0 : v_1 : \cdots : v_k : \lambda_{k+1}],[n_0 : n_1 : \cdots : n_k : \lambda_{k+1}]]$

$[[v_0 : \lambda_1 : \cdots : \lambda_k : v_{k+1}],[n_0 : \lambda_1 : \cdots : \lambda_k : n_{k+1}]]$
$[[v_0 : \lambda_{1/k} : v_{k+1}],[n_0 : \lambda_{1/k} : n_{k+1}]]$ *(shortly)*

Q.E.D.

2.5 Restoring Sentences

The Spanish language has an **SVO** structure (*Subject-Verb-Object*) [23]. The **S** and **O** are cores closely related with nominal categories, whereas the **V** core is associated to verbal categories. Hence, for simplicity purposes and without losing generality, the **SVO** structure can be seen as an NVN sequence where N corresponds to a sequence of *nominal cores* and V corresponds to a *verbal core*. In this subsection, a function capable of restoring *well-formed sentences* from the *algebraic space* is defined.

Definition 7 (Structurally well-formed Spanish sentences [SWFSS]).
*Let us denote **SWFSS** the **NVN** sequences or any of these variants: **N**, **NV**, **VN**, and **NVN**. Some examples of these sequences include: NVNV, NVNVNVN, VNVNVN, etc.*

Definition 8 (Function $F_{\bar{O}_v}$). *Let $F_{\bar{O}_v}$ be a function that maps members of $\bar{O}_v$ into **SWFSS**. Table 2 shows the mapping process. The blank space is represented by the symbol ƀ.*

Table 2. Function $F_{\bar{O}_v}$

$[\![X]\!]$	$F_{\bar{O}_v}([\![X]\!])$
$[\![[\lambda_{0/m}][N_{0/m}]]\!]$	$\lambda_0 b n_0 b \cdots b \lambda_m b n_m$
$[\![[V_{0/m}][\lambda_{0/m}]]\!]$	$\lambda_0 b \lambda_1 b \cdots b \lambda_m$
$[\![[V_{i/m}],[N_{i/m}]]\!]$	$v_i b n_i \cdots v_j b n_j \cdots v_m b n_m$
$[\![[\lambda_{i/j} : V_{j+1/m}],[N_{i/m}]]\!]$	$\lambda_i b n_i b \lambda_{i+1} b n_{i+1} \cdots v_{j+1} b n_{j+1} \cdots v_m b n_m$
Special cases	
$[\![[\lambda_{i/j} : V_{j+1/k}],[N_{i/k-1} : \lambda_k]]\!]$	$\lambda_i b n_i b \lambda_{i+1} b n_{i+1} \cdots b v_{j+1} b n_{j+1} \cdots b v_k b \lambda_k$
$[\![[V_{i/k}],[N_{i/k-1} : \lambda_k]]\!]$	$v_i b n_i b \cdots b v_k b \lambda_k$

Theorem 2. *All expressions in the set $\bar{\Theta}$ are **SWFSS**.*

Proof. If an expression in the Spanish language meets Definition 7 then it is considered **SWFSS**. Table 3 shows the structure of a sentence by applying the function $F_{\bar{O}_v}$. Each possible outcome meets the requirements of a **SWFSS**. Q.E.D.

Hence, an implementation of the function $F_{\bar{O}_v}$ can rebuild structurally well-formed sentences from the *algebraic space*.

Table 3. Structure of a sentence by applying the $F_{\bar{O}_v}$ mapping

$F_{\bar{O}_v}([\![X]\!])$	Sentence structure	Type
$\lambda_0 bn_0 b \cdots b \lambda_m bn_m$	$n_0\ n_1\ \cdots\ n_m$	**N**
$\lambda_0 b \lambda_1 b \cdots b \lambda_m$	λ	*null*
$v_i bn_i \cdots v_j bn_j \cdots v_m bn_m$	$v_i\ n_i\ \cdots\ v_j\ n_j\ \cdots\ v_m\ n_m$	**VNVN**
$\lambda_i bn_i b \lambda_{i+1} bn_{i+1} \cdots v_{j+1} bn_{j+1} \cdots v_m bn_m$	$n_i\ n_{i+1}\ \cdots\ v_{j+1}\ n_{j+1}\ \cdots\ v_m\ n_m$	**NVNVN**
Special cases		
$\lambda_i bn_i b \lambda_{i+1} bn_{i+1} \cdots bv_{j+1} bn_{j+1} \cdots bv_k b \lambda_k$	$n_i\ n_{i+1}\ \cdots\ v_{j+1}\ n_{j+1}\ \cdots\ v_k$	**NVNV**
$v_i bn_i b \cdots bv_k b \lambda_k$	$v_i\ n_i\ \cdots\ v_k$	**VNV**

2.6   Semantics and Sub-groups

The meaning of a sentence generated by $F_{\bar{O}_v}$ must be maintained. However, this function $F_{\bar{O}_v}$ can not guarantee it completely, e.g., if the elements e_1 and e_4 shown in Fig. 2 are operated to generate a new member, then the result will be:

$$[\![[v_1], [n_1]]\!] \oplus_v [\![[\lambda_4], [n_4]]\!] = [\![[v_1 : \lambda_{2/4}], [n_1 : \lambda_{2/3} : n_4]]\!]$$

By applying $F_{\bar{O}_v}$, the outcome would be the following sentence: *"programada para el próximo 26 de marzo la Paz y la justicia"* whose meaning, although it is syntactically correct, is confusing.

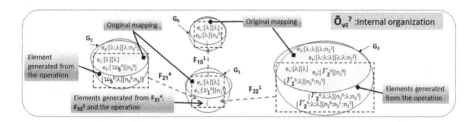

Fig. 3. A sentence mapping with the organizations inside of the set $\bar{O}_v$

The problem can be solved by dividing the set $\bar{O}_v$ into sub-groups and establishing a hierarchy between them through functions. Figure 3 shows a possible reorganization in $\bar{O}_v$. The mapping between sets works as a cascade effect from the chosen core up to the root. Each function inserts λ-elements to the left hand for each member mapped, thenceforth, the operation $\oplus_v$ is applied between the mapped element and a *key-element*(**head-v**) which is the only verb belonging to the codomain. Additionally, the only elements mapped are those embedded in the dashed box. For example, applying the function $F_{21}^4(e_5)$ lead the following procedure:

$$e_5 = [\![[v_5 0], [n_5 0]]\!] \Rightarrow e_5^{21} = [\![[\lambda_{0/3} : v_{50}^{21}], [\lambda_{0/3} : n_{50}^{21}]]\!]$$
$$\Rightarrow e_5^{21} \oplus_v e_{1-k} = [\![[v_1 0 : \lambda_{1/3} : v_{50}^{21}], [n_1 0 : \lambda_{1/3} : n_{50}^{21}]]\!]$$
$$\Rightarrow (e_5^{21} \oplus_v e_1)^{10} \oplus_v e_{0-k} = [\![[\lambda : (v_1 0)^{10} : \lambda_{2/4} : (v_5^{21})^{10}], [n_0 : (n_1 0)^1 : \lambda_{2/4} : (n_5^{21})^{10}]]\!]$$

The function's superscript indicates the number of λ-elements to be inserted, and the superscript of the e_i-elements indicates the function that mapped them. In this case, the result would be: "*La marcha programada, para el próximo 26 de marzo, recibía críticas*". It is noteworthy that all source text of the sentences must be consistent which is convenient because a restored sentence from this text is also consistent.

3   Implementing the Model

The implementation has been focused on finding the limits of the cores and building the algebraic space. First of all, a framework was built with a layered architecture which was instantiated to process texts in Spanish. The most relevant layers of the framework are the following: *language recognition*, *planning*, and *reaction*. The first layer was designed to identify the language of the text and to divide it into sentences which will be sent to the next layer one at a time. The second layer chooses the applications that should be executed to dissociate a sentence and to initialize the model sets. The last layer executes the applications chosen by the planner. The framework also includes a main module for control and instantiation of the layers.

The *reaction* layer executes several *heuristics* to process only texts in the Spanish language; it was divided into three phases. In the first phase, each sentence is processed by a *linguistic tool*, commanded by **VISL**[2] parser [22]. The second phase, named *classifier*, receives from the parser output a very extensive word classification to reduce its number in a new set. In the third phase, called *packer*, the *cores* are created. This process involves a loop where neighboring words (or clusters) are operated to be packed into a single class that can be a *nominal core*, a *determinant*, or a *verbal core*. *Cores* are saved in a database by creating the sets of the model.

A *verbal core* category introduces a *sequence of cores* that ends where a new *verbal core* starts or when the sentence ends. *Verbal cores* are used to establish hierarchies between subgroups where each one of them has a *verbal core* designated as the *head-v* (see Subsect. 2.6). Such hierarchy depends on these characteristics of the *head-v*: a *main verbal-core* (**main-v**), a *subordinated verbal-core* (**subord-w**), and an *optional verbal-core* (**opt-V**). The **main-v** subgroups are arranged in a vector which is ordered by the *head-v*-subscripts; the vector is the

---

[2] The **VISL** parser, from the *University of Southern Denmark* was used in this work under the permission of this institution.

root of the hierarchy and any other category or subcategory will be subordinated to any one of its elements.

The **opt-V** subcategory introduces a *sequence of cores* that is considered optional, i.e., if a subgroup contains a *head-v* with the **opt-V** subcategory, its information is considered non-essential to the restoration sentence process. The **opt-V** category scope in a sentence ends where a new *verbal core* with category **subord-w** or **main-v** starts.

The **subord-w** class introduces a *sequence of cores* subordinated with regard to the **main-v** subcategory which is present immediately after in the sentence. Additionally, if several **subord-w** groups appear before the **main-v** group, they will form a subordinated **subord-w**-vector. The combination **subord-w** + **main-v** forms a special unit since all the information contained is essential to preserving the meaning.

The *determinants* separates two *nominal cores* or, introduces a *nominal core sequence* after a *verbal core*. As well as the *verbal cores*, they have a subclassification that labels them as: *preposition determinant* (**prep-d**), *conjunction determinant* (**conj-d**), *disjunction determinant* (**comma-d**), and *optional determinant* (**opt-d**). The (**prep-d**) and (**opt-d**) types introduce a *nominal-cores sequence*, but the sequence introduced by the latter is optional (see **opt-V** above). The (**conj-d**) is a *determinant* that suggests combining the *nominal-cores sequence* that it introduces with the previous *nominal-cores sequence* for proper understanding. On the other hand, the **comma-d** determinant suggests separation, i.e., the *nominal core* introduced starts a new sub-sentence inside of the sentence. The sub-sentence ends when a new (**conj-d**) or a (**opt-d**) starts, or the sentence ends. An example of this implementation is shown in the Sect. 2.6. The group G_2 is subordinated with regard to G_1, and the group G_3 contains optional information.

3.1 Results of the Sentence Dissociation and Generation of the Sets

The processes of *dissociation* and *generation of the sets* were tested with three types of corpora: Entertainment, Tourism, and News. Table 4 shows the statistics of the creation of the subsets belonging to the *Cartesian product* which will be mapped into the *algebraic space* and the resulting errors of the process. The $<v, n>$ column represents the number of subgroups that are created in the *algebraic space* without considering their type within the hierarchy or the sentence where it comes from. The second and third columns show two types of *nominal cores*; the first one is the set whose subject is explicit inside of the core, while in the second one corresponds to an anaphoric subject. The analysis of the implementation is focuses on three types of errors that can occurs in the execution in the layers execution. The possible errors are: *parsing error*, *compacting error*, and *false-positive error*.

The *parsing error* is generated by the *syntactic parser* when it cannot properly classify the words of the sentence. In this case, this type of error was minimal because the tool is very robust, and it has been tested exhaustively. The *compacting error* is associated with the effectiveness of the *classifier's* heuristics which

Table 4. Statistics related to the creation of cores

	Subsets of VxN			Type of errors in cores					Total Number of Sentences
<v,n>	**<n,λ>**		S-CP %	Parser Error	Compact Error	False Positives	FP %	
	Subject	Anaphora						
Entertainment_1	76	47	173	89%	4	15	17	5%	332
Entertainment_2	15	12	31	89%	1	0	6	9%	65
Tourism_1	143	28	144	97%	3	2	5	2%	325
Tourism_2	57	16	53	98%	2	0	0	0%	128
Tourism_3	54	6	62	98%	1	0	2	2%	125
News_1	40	23	43	97%	0	1	2	2%	109
News_2	24	7	26	89%	2	0	5	8%	64
News_3	49	16	43	93%	2	1	5	4%	116

can be influenced by the *parsing error*. The *false-positive error* represents the errors occurred during the *dissociation process* and *set generation*, and it is the most significant type of error. The generation of cores depends on the *parsing* and the *classifier* processes. The value of the *false-positive error* is slightly superior in comparison to the previous errors which shows the successfulness of the heuristic system. The worst-case scenario occurs in a small corpus marked by a 9% error. This a small loss of sentences is not significant enough to compromise the main idea of the text, because the rest of the sentences can fully support it. In general, the processes of *dissociation* and the *set generation* delivered good results.

4   Conclusions and Future Work

The main goal of this research is to generate a space where query-based processes will be performed in natural language, and the decision-making task could be carried out by creating small theories based on sentences restored from several sources along with the query sentence. Such approach would cause a reduction in the performance of the selecting and the decision-making activities. In first place, this can be explained by the fact that the search is improved by enabling the creation of sets both inside of a sentence and between sentences (hierarchies), and even between texts. In second place, although there are several tools to convert texts into theories or ontologies, the process of restoring sentences would reduce the number of sentences that can form a query-based small theory. This contributes to tasks such as the construction of the theory which could be created dynamically, and the performance of decision-making process.

This paper introduces two main processes that could be useful for generating of small theories free from inconsistencies. The use case scenarios involved sentences in Spanish. The first process divides the sentences into cores in order to map them into an *algebraic space* where they can be manipulated and reprocessed. Its implementation was achieved with good results. The other process refers to the (complete or partial) restoration of a sentence by mapping elements from the algebraic space to a linguistic space by ensuring syntactically and structurally well-formed sentences, and that the meanings can be guaranteed with some rearrangements of the sets in the algebraic space. Regarding future work along this line of research, the anaphora could be implemented to establish links between cores from different sentences.

In summary, a new model based on open-use Mathematics was proposed, and an implementation of the *dissociation and generation of the sets* was implemented with good results. The generated repository contains several sets that form *Abelian groups*. Finally, a rearrangement of the groups for the Spanish language was suggested which safekeeps the structure and the meaning of the sentences restored from the algebraic space. This approach could have several uses such as in search engines since the information is saved in its original format (text), and the decision related to a specific topic would be generated by satisfying small theories dynamically created through the interaction between the repository and the queries.

References

1. Kecskes, I.: The paradox of communications. Socio-cognitive approach to pragmatics. Inf. Control., 52–55 (2010)
2. Tulving, E.: Episodic and semantic memory. In: Tulving, E., Donaldson, W. (eds.) Organization of Memory, pp. 381–403. Academic Press, New York (1972)
3. Havel, I.M.: Strategies of Remembrance: From Pindar to Hölderlin, chap. 2. Cambridge Scholars (2009)
4. Conway, M., Pleydell-Pearce, C.: The construction of autobiographical memories in the self memory system. Psychol. Rev. **107**(2), 261–288 (2000)
5. Bazire, M., Brézillon, P.: Understanding Context before using it. In: Dey, A., Kokinov, B., Leake, D., Turner, R. (eds.) CONTEXT 2005. LNCS (LNAI), vol. 3554, pp. 29–40. Springer, Heidelberg (2005). https://doi.org/10.1007/11508373_3
6. Buvac, S., Mason, I.A.: Propositional logic of context. In: AAAI, pp. 412–419 (1993)
7. McCarthy, J.: Notes on formalizing context. In: Proceedings of the 13th International Joint Conference on Artifical Intelligence, San Francisco, CA, USA, pp. 555–560 (1993)
8. Guha, R.: Contexts: a formalization and some applications (1992)
9. Ghidini, C., Giunchiglia, F.: Local models semantics, or contextual reasoning=locality+compatibility. Artif. Intell. **127**(2), 221–259 (2001). https://doi.org/10.1016/S0004-3702(01)00064-9
10. Haase, P., et al.: D3.1.1 context languages - state of the art. Technical report D3.1.1, Universität Karlsruhe (TH) (2006)
11. Costanza, P., Hirschfeld, R.: Language constructs for context-oriented programming: an overview of contextl. In: Proceedings of the 2005 Symposium on Dynamic Languages, New York, NY, USA, pp. 1–10 (2005)

12. Salvaneschi, G., Ghezzi, C., Pradella, M.: Context-oriented programming: A software engineering perspective. J. Syst. Softw. **85**(8), 1801–1817 (2012). https://doi.org/10.1016/j.jss.2012.03.024
13. Luna Traill, E., Vigueras Avila, A., Baez Pinal, G.E.: Diccionario básico de lingüística. UNAM (2005)
14. Vivaldi, G.M., Sánchez, A.: Curso de Redacción. Thomson Eds, Paraninfo S.A. (2000)
15. Gruber, T.R.: Toward principles for the design of ontologies used for knowledge sharing. Int. J. Hum. Comput. Stud. **43**(5–6), 907–928 (1995). https://doi.org/10.1006/ijhc.1995.1081
16. Cimiano, P., Völker, J.: Text2onto - a framework for ontology learning and data-driven change discovery. In: Proceedings of the 10th International Conference on Applications of Natural Language to Information Systems (NLDB), Alicante, Spain, pp. 227–238 (2005)
17. Velardi, P., Faralli, S., Navigli, R.: Ontolearn reloaded: a graph-based algorithm for taxonomy induction. Comput. Linguist. **39**(3), 665–707 (2013). http://dblp.uni-trier.de/db/journals/coling/coling39.html#VelardiFN13
18. Lenat, D.B., Guha, R.V.: Building Large Knowledge-Based Systems; Representation and Inference in the Cyc Project. Addison-Wesley Longman Publishing Co., Inc., Boston (1989)
19. Arroyo Cantón, C., Berlato Rodríguez, P.: La comunicación. Lengua castellana y Literatura. Oxford University Press, España (2012)
20. Montealegre, R.: La comprension del texto: Sentido y significado. Revista Latinoamericana de Psicología. Universidad Nacional de Colombia **36**(2), 243–255 (2004)
21. González Calvo, J.M.: Los conceptos de proposición, oración y enunciado. La frase nominal. Liceus Servicios de Gestión y Comunicación S.L (2006)
22. Bick, E.: A constraint grammar-based parser for spanish. In: TIL (2006)
23. Boeree, G.: Basic language structures (2017). http://webspace.ship.edu/cgboer/basiclangstruct.html

HOMSI, a Home-Office Model for the Software Industry in the Big Cities of Mexico

José Sergio Ruíz Castilla[(⊠)], Jair Cervantes Canales,
Dolores Arévalo Zenteno, and José Hernández Santiago

Universidad Autónoma del Estado de México,
Centro Universitario UAEM Texcoco, Av. Jardín Zumpango,
s/n. Fracc. el Tejocote, 56259 Texcoco, Estado de México, Mexico
jsergioruizc@gmail.com, chazarral7@gmail.com,
darevaloz@gmail.com,
jose_hernandez_santiago@hotmail.com

Abstract. The Software Industry in Mexico (SIM) is accentuated in large cities. This industry requires thousands of employees who must go to the offices weekdays. However, mobility in large cities is increasingly complicated by two factors: the first is the distance from your residence to the office, that can be from 1 to 30 km away or more, on the other hand, the expenses caused by the transport. The means of transport can be from the worker himself or public transport as: metro, bus, "metrobus", taxi, etc. In this work, a home-office model is proposed, which suggests that developers go once to the main office and the rest of the weekdays work from your home. The above, is not by default, because they must have the minimum conditions to work in his own house. However, when working in their own home there are benefits such as: saving time and money in the travel and on the other hand, the developer does not suffer stress caused by the daily travel. In the model, a central office is proposed for meetings and training. So that, each developer must have a space in her own home and adapted for a home office. The above, implies having an Uninterrupted Communication Medium (UCM) to be in contact between developers, as well as with the Couch (Co) and the Project Manager (PM). In the results, statistics of travel times and expenses, as well as the effects of traveling to work every day, are shown. We conclude that, the Home-Office Model can achieve more satisfied developers; less stressed can increases productivity in organizations that develop software.

Keywords: Home-Office · Model · Software · Software projects ·
Software industry · Developers

1 Introduction

1.1 Context of Companies that Develop Software

In Mexico there are great cities such as: Mexico City, Guadalajara, Monterrey, Puebla, Querétaro, etc. in which Software Industry exists. Due to the size of the cities, there are mobility problems that cause software developers to invest a lot of time in the travel as

© Springer Nature Switzerland AG 2019
M. Botto-Tobar et al. (Eds.): ICCCE 2018, CCIS 959, pp. 87–97, 2019.
https://doi.org/10.1007/978-3-030-12018-4_7

well as disbursing a significant part of their salary in transport. The Home-office modality tends to grow, however, there is no reference framework to make the most of this modality.

The home-office mode looks for scenarios in large cities such as Mexico City, which, according to Moovit, up to 30% of workers make a trip of more than two hours to go to and from work, in turn, they are required 88 min to move on a weekday. On the other hand, they need to travel up to 9.9 km on average and at least 28% travel more than 12 km [1]. Another study by Schafer and Victor found that a person spends 1.1 h per day per travel, so in a large city rapid transport systems are required [9], however the development of this type of transport is limited to resources and design of the cities, such is the case of Mexico City.

The home office is not only a space but a place adapted to work with all the physical and even virtual elements to maintain a working environment of the work team [2].

Other factors such as lighting are really important because they directly influence the productivity of the developer. Natural light is ideal to avoid eyestrain, when natural light is not possible, then intelligent lighting must exist [3]. However, workers can have the same behavior of energy use in their home as in the office [4], so the developer should have good habits in the use of energy to not affect their economy by implementing the model of Home-office.

The social and family aspect of the worker can be affected when the worker works in a virtual office or at home, as revealed by the IBM study comparing a traditional office, virtual office and a home office. It can influence aspects of: job performance, work motivation, job retention and career opportunity, success in workload, life and personal and family success. Perceptions, direct comparisons and multivariate analyzes suggest that the influence of the virtual office is mostly positive in aspects of work, but somewhat negative in aspects of personal/family life. The influence of the central office seems to be mostly positive and the influence of the traditional office mostly negative in aspects of work and personal/life [5].

The aspect of information security is undoubtedly to be taken into account, because developers, from the office at home, must comply with and implement measures that allow the security of the information they store and transmit to the contracted cloud, for the organization [6]. In this case, each home office must have the same level of security as the main office, as well as maintain communication channels that allow the exchange of information with other elements of the work team and encourage interaction [7].

The information of the projects must be in the cloud to achieve accessibility by the developers of their office, taking advantage of the benefits of storage in the cloud that is used from education [8], for companies, among other important uses.

The hours that you must work from the home office must be those corresponding to the traditional office, however, in Latin America too many hours are worked [10] so, the developer should only cover the hours determined in his contract so as not to affect the relationship with their families and with their health. Work long hours can affect the health of the worker according to Spurgeon, Harrignton and Cooper in the European Union the worker can oppose to work more than 48 h a week, however, in other cases and places like Latin America the days may be longer 50 h a week. The above affects the worker in possible effects on health and performance. It is concluded that there is currently enough evidence to raise concerns about the health risks and safety of long working hours. However, much more work is required to define the level and nature of these risks [11].

The purpose of this paper is to propose a Model that allows defining how to implement the Home-office mode in the large cities of Mexico. It is intended that the model contributes to the implementation of Home Office in the Software Industry. Researchers living in Mexico City and in the periphery were investigated, finding times of transfers and resources necessary for their mobility.

2 Materials and Methods

The model focuses on organizations that develop software projects through one or more work teams. The model combines Home Office (HO) with other environments: client-analyst, user-developer, trainer-developer, developer-developer, among others. Therefore, the model is considered mixed, on the one hand, tasks are carried out in the Project Office (PO) such as meetings to analyze strategies and agreements and on the other hand, work in HO by each developer. Without omitting that, they must be connected uninterruptedly by some means such as: mobile telephony, email, social networks, among other means. The previous Uninterrupted Communication Media (UCM) must be duly established in each organization.

The Project Activities (PA) will be carried out in the APO and in the AHO of the developers, so, there must be a strategy of integration of tasks in a server, but much better in the cloud. Therefore, it can be determined that the PA results from the sum of the activities carried out in the APO and the AHOs. See formula 1.

$$PA = (APO_1 + APO_2 + APO_3, \ldots APO_n) + (AHO_1 + AHO_2 + AHO_3, \ldots AHO_n) \quad (1)$$

Where PA are the activities of the project; APO are the activities carried out in the APOs; and AHO are the activities carried out in the AHOs of the developers.

2.1 Assignment of Tasks

The Assignment of Tasks (AT) will be carried out by the Project Manager (PM) in the APO or through the UCM. Each task must be defined and estimated in man-hours in order to establish the dates and times of delivery. Whereas each organization defines the hours to work per week.

It is recommended that the AT be weekly, preferably on Mondays in a meeting in the APO under a detailed work plan that defines tasks and times of completion. The above in order to know the dates and times of delivery of each task. Other tasks may be assigned at any day and time through an UCM. The Model that has been called HOMSI is proposed. See Fig. 1.

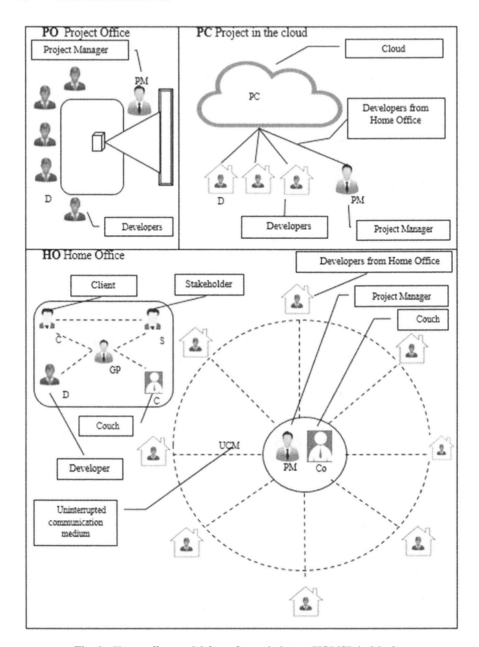

Fig. 1. Home office model for software industry (HOMSI) in Mexico.

2.2 Delivery of Deliverables

The deliverables are products of a task such as: text files, forms, designs, programming codes, reports, test results, etc. Once the developer finishes a task, he must send it on the date and before the established time through an UCM. The sending of new tasks to the developer, as well as the delivery of deliverables by the developer, must be at previously agreed working hours, considering regional schedules if there are developers who live in different time zones. Therefore, each AT must have the following elements. Formula 2.

$$AT = (T, ETHT, D, Ti) \tag{2}$$

Where AT is the assignment of tasks, T is the task assigned to the developer, ETHT is the Estimated Time in Hours of the Task for the completion, D is the date and Ti is the time of sending.

There should be rules or policies to establish situations in which a developer will not work or send a deliverable out of time. For example, to notify at least 2 days before, the previous thing so that the PM carries out a new AT or adjustment to the plan of the Project.

2.3 Communication with the Work Team and Coach

The developers will be working from their HO, however they must be "connected" with the PM and the Couch at all times (it is recommended that the organization have it). In the same way, they can be connected with one or several fellow developers. The communication is a priority for some clarification or doubt and also for questions of socialization.

2.4 Home Office

The HO must have minimum conditions for the developer. The parameters are 6 to 9 m^2 independent of the rest of the house, with a door and a window for natural light and ventilation. With natural or adequate lighting, climate and noise under control. Table 1 details the characteristics of the HO space.

Table 1. Ideal characteristics of space of the HO.

Element	Characteristics
Space	6 to 9 m^2 Whit door and window Independent of the rest of the house
Illumination	Natural light or white light
Noise	It must be minimum or controllable
Temperature	From 19 to 26° centigrade
Colors	The colors of the walls should be clear avoiding: blue, orange, red and black
Furniture	A desk or work table of at least 120 by 180 cm A semi-executive or executive chair with backrest, height adjustment and wheels
Equipment	A desktop or laptop computer with at least 24-in. screen Printer, scanner, stapler, clips, white sheets, folders, pens, pencils, among other stationery items
Internet	It must have Internet connection preferably broadband

The work schedules should be the same as the PO to maintain communication under the same hours. The developer should not work more hours than his normal shift that must correspond to the schedule established by the organization, to avoid fatigue and exhaustion. Also, avoid eating at the HO at any time, but establish a meal schedule as if you were in the PO.

Hours worked (HW) in the HO must be accumulated during the week until completing a schedule established by the organization. In this case the weekly hours WH must coincide with the Estimated Hours of the Tasks Assigned EHTA. See formula 3.

$$WH = EHTA_1 + EHTA_2 + \ldots EHTA_n \tag{3}$$

2.5   Expenses of the Project Office

The Expenses of the Project Office (EPO) will decrease due to the fact that there is not a paid work space for the development of the project. The costs of electricity, rent, security and hygiene will be paid respectively by the developers. However, who should pay the Expenses of the Home Office (EHO)? The company cannot pay for them, because they would have to generate individualized invoices for each developer, in addition to that, the expenses would rise, because they would be maintaining multiple offices instead of just one.

The model recommends an office with reception, a private cubicle and a meeting room. Whereas, the office can be shared or rented for hours or days. For example, on Monday mornings.

The expenses of the EPO home office are determined considering the elements of formula 4.

$$EPO = R + E + W + I + SH \tag{4}$$

Where EPO is the expenses of the project office, R is the rent, E is electricity, W is the water, I is the internet service and SH is the safety and hygiene.

The other option only corresponds to a rent of one day or n hours of a shared office. In this case the only expense is the rent payment that already includes the services.

2.6   Expenses of the Home Office

The Expenses of the Home Office EHO are generated by the consumption of electricity, water and internet, as well as safety and hygiene. In this case, the developer will pay for it along with the expenses of his house. So who should pay the EHO? In the model, it is proposed that the company grant a bonus to the developer to offset said payments. Formula 5 shows the origin of EHO.

$$EHO = P \times (E + I + W + SH) \tag{5}$$

Where EHO is the expenses of the home office, P is the percentage corresponding to the expenses of the office space, E is electricity, I is the internet service, W is the water service and SH is the security and hygiene

2.7   Travel Times

The Travel Time of the Developers (TTD) involves the trip from your home to the office and vice versa, see formula 6.

$$TTD = THO + TOH \tag{6}$$

Where TTD is the developer's Travel time in one day, THO is the time from your home to the office and TOH is the Travel time from the office to your home. In this case, not all developers take the same because it depends on where they live. So, formula 7 shows us the time of the entire team.

$$TTWT = TTD_1 + TTD_2 + TTD_3 \ldots TTD_n \tag{7}$$

Where TTWT is the Time of Travel of the Work Team and TTD is the time of travel of each member of the work team. Therefore, TTWT is obtained from the time of each one of the members of the work team. Finally, it is necessary to calculate the type of travel during the project. Whereas, a project lasts n effective days, it is possible to calculate the total time with formula 8.

$$TTT = TTWT * NDDP \tag{8}$$

Where TTT is the Total Time of Travels of the entire work team during the duration of the project, TTWT is the Travel time of the work team and NDDP is the Number of Days of Duration of the Project.

The travel time does not directly impact the project, but should be considered, absences and delays due to problems during the travel, as well as stress and fatigue of the team members. In the case of a developer who lives two or more hours away from the office, he will have less time for rest and recreation.

2.8   Travel Expenses

Expenses for travels involve fuel, tolls and parking (if the developer uses a car) while those using public transport involve metro, bus or taxi payments. So, the daily expenditure of a developer is shown with the formula 9.

$$TED = TEHO + TEOH \tag{9}$$

Where TED is the Travel Expenses of a Developer, TEHO is the cost of moving the house to the office while TEOH is the cost of moving the office to the home. Whereas, you could take another route or type of public transportation. Therefore, there is a travel fee for the entire work team as shown with formula 10.

$$EWTT = TED_1 + TED_2 + TED_3 \ldots TED_n \qquad (10)$$

Where EWTT are the Expenses of Work Team Travels and TED is the travel cost of each developer considering that each has its own travel cost. Therefore, there is a total expenditure and travels reflected in formula 11.

$$TET = EWTT * NDDP \qquad (11)$$

Where TET are the Total Expenses of Travels of the entire work team during the project. EWTT is the Expenses of Work Team Travels and NDDP is the Number of Days of Duration of the Project.

Similarly, the travel costs do not directly impact the project, but the developers that part of their income is spent on the travel, demanding better compensation to the company. With this model could be reduced by up to 80% to avoid going to the office weekdays.

2.9 Knowledge Management

The best way to transfer knowledge is face-to-face thanks to the interaction in the workspace. In this proposed model, the transfer of knowledge can be affected because the interaction through the UCM has certain limitations. Therefore, it is recommended to encourage interaction in meetings and training.

It is also recommended to use communication systems that allow to connect several users simultaneously so that during the day they can communicate between colleagues.

2.10 Tools for HOMSI Communication

An UCM is required to allow the work team to communicate with each other through the internet network. As well as, the developers with the Project Manager and the Couch. In the same way, the Project Manager with the client and the stakeholders. For what is recommended there is an UCM that guarantees communication at all times. In the market there are tools for this purpose from e-mail exprofeso tools such as: Google Groups, Skype, Cloud computing, among others.

2.11 HOMSI in Mexico

For the purpose of testing the HOMSI model, we research with developers in the software industry of the Mexico City, we designed an instrument for get information about the developers which are in the software development. We got 84 answers of developers which traveled daily a big city. With questions about of travel expenses and travel times. We include a men and women of different ages. On big and small organizations. With the data we did analysis and we find results which are presented in the next section.

3   Results and Discussion

3.1   Space of Home Office

The days that 84 developers worked from 4 to 6 days. Although, most work 5 days a 77% there is a percentage of 16% that works 6 days and also a 7% four days, as can be seen in Fig. 2.

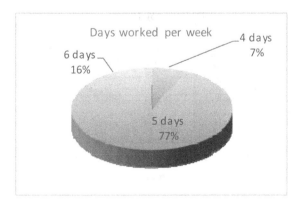

Fig. 2. Days worked per week in Mexico.

The time of travels from the developer's house to the office goes from 0 to 15 min to 121 to 180 min. In this case, the largest number of developers requires 91 to 180 min, as shown in Fig. 3. The transfer time is very similar to round travel and return. The total time of transfer is the sum of go and return that can be from 30 min to 6 h.

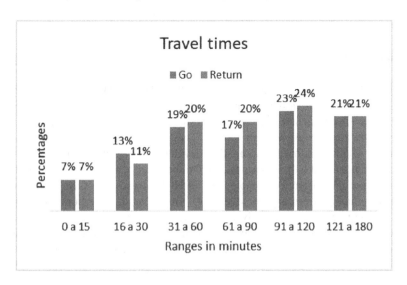

Fig. 3. Travels times for developers to and from work in Mexico.

Another important variable is the expense of travel from your home to the office and vice versa. In this case, the expenses converted to dollars as of April 18, 2018 are presented. Expenses can range from 0 to 3 dollars to 11 to 17 dollars. In this case, the travel expenses are concentrated in 6 dollars as can be seen in Fig. 4. In this case, the expenses are concentrated from 0 to 6 dollars.

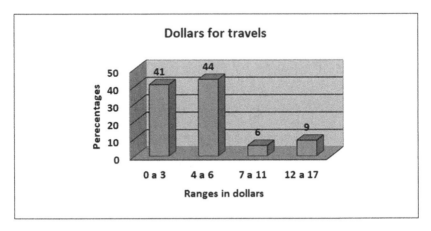

Fig. 4. Cost in dollars of travels of the developers in Mexico City.

Of the developers surveyed only 38% have a space of 6 to 9 m^2 to adapt an office, however, 80% have internet at home. The above indicates that in Mexico we still do not have the optimal conditions for home-office.

The transfer of the developers affects them mainly in "Tiredness and exhaustion" to 54%. So, it can affect the developer in the daily activities.

4   Conclusions

There are traditional offices, virtual and Home-office. Traditional offices are decreasing, while virtual offices and Home Office are on the rise. Home-office mode is a trend in our days, because organizations seek to minimize their office costs. On the other hand, the travels are getting slower and longer. The proposed model HOMSI defines a framework under which organizations that develop software can work. It was found that, travels range from half an hour to 3 h. On the other hand, expenses range from 3 to 6 dollars per day. Therefore, implementing HOMSI can save time and money, in addition to reducing stress on developers. It is important that the home office should have good lighting, low noise, privacy, Internet connection, security in the internet network, among other factors. It is expected that, in the future, more organizations will implement Home-office, improving their productivity and employee satisfaction.

References

1. Aplicación de movilidad. https://moovitapp.com/insights/es-419/Moovit_Insights_%C3% 8Dndice_de_Transporte_P%C3%BAblico_M%C3%A9xico_Ciudad_de_Mexico-822?utm_ source=seo_pages. Accessed 16 Apr 2018

2. Honda, S., Okada, K., Matsushita, Y.: A home office system based on a virtual shared room: an environment corresponding to degree of concentration. In: Masunaga, Y., Katayama, T., Tsukamoto, M. (eds.) WWCA 1998. LNCS, vol. 1368, pp. 364–380. Springer, Heidelberg (1998). https://doi.org/10.1007/3-540-64216-1_61

3. Mocanu, A.: An argumentative approach to smart home office ambient lighting. In: Ivanović, M., Bădică, C., Dix, J., Jovanović, Z., Malgeri, M., Savić, M. (eds.) IDC 2017. SCI, vol. 737, pp. 225–234. Springer, Cham (2018). https://doi.org/10.1007/978-3-319-66379-1_20

4. Littleford, C., Ryley, T.J., Firth, S.K.: Context control and the spillover of energy use behaviours between office and home settings. J. Environ. Psychol. 40, 157–166 (2014)

5. Hill, E.J., Ferris, M., Märtinson, V.: Does it matter where you work? A comparison of how three work venues (traditional office, virtual office, and home office) influence aspects of work and personal/family life. J. Vocat. Behav. 63(2), 220–241 (2003)

6. Winder, D.: Securing your home office. Infosecurity 7(6), 21–23 (2010)

7. Fulton, C.: Control of information in the virtual office: preparation of intermediaries to facilitate the exchange of information in the home work environment. New Univers. Libr. 103(6), 209–215 (2002). https://doi.org/10.1108/03074800210729665

8. Sultan, N.: Cloud computing for education: a new dawn? Int. J. Inf. Manag. 30(2), 109–116 (2010)

9. Schafer, A., Victor, D.G.: The future mobility of the world population. Transp. Res. Part A Policy Pract. 34(3), 171–205 (2000)

10. Huberman, M., Minns, C.: The times they are not changin': days and hours of work in Old and New Worlds, 1870–2000. Explor. Econ. Hist. 44(4), 538–567 (2007). https://doi.org/10.1016/j.eeh.2007.03.002

11. Spurgeon, A., Harrington, J.M., Cooper, C.L.: Health and safety problems associated with long working hours: a review of the current position. Occup. Environ. Med. 54(6). http://dx.doi.org/10.1136/oem.54.6.367. BMJ Journal

Using a Machine Learning Logistic Regression Algorithm to Classify Nanomedicine Clinical Trials in a Known Repository

Charles M. Pérez-Espinoza[1]([⊠]), Nuvia Beltran-Robayo[1],
Teresa Samaniego-Cobos[1], Abel Alarcón-Salvatierra[1],
Ana Rodriguez-Mendez[1], and Paola Jaramillo-Barreiro[2]

[1] Universidad Agraria del Ecuador, Guayaquil, Ecuador
{cperez,nbeltran,tsamaniego,jalarcon,
arodriguez}@uagraria.edu.ec
[2] Universidad Laica Vicente Rocafuerte, Guayaquil, Ecuador
pjaramillo@capecomworld.com

Abstract. Today, the nanotechnology is the most critical technology that helps in many scientific advances, because this science allows us to work with molecular structures and their atoms, obtaining material that acts chemical and biologically different to those manifesting in bigger longitudes. Many sciences join nanotechnology to improve their researches, and one of them is medicine. In nanomedicine, many researchers are looking for a way to obtain information about these nanometric materials to enhance their studies that lead in many occasions to prove these methods or to create a new compound that helps modern medicine against dominant diseases. Years after years the world increase trials with these nanomaterials and in this work the authors are going to demonstrate this issue, using the clinical trials repository in one of the most famous trials web pages. Many scientists that work with these trials, wish to obtain only the ones those that need, but in these repositories, they have to search and read each one to make sure that the trial is about what they are researching. The authors implement an application for build a train model that involved a new method of pre-processing text to classify through logistic regression in these trials. For this classification, the authors downloaded an entire database (www.clinicaltrials.gov) and used nanoinformatic with an artificial intelligence machine learning supervised algorithm to classify them. The authors classified trials that are about nanomedicine and trials that not. And finally present the results of the number of clinical trials that are about nanomedicine.

Keywords: Nanotechnology · Nanomedicine · Nanoinformatics ·
Machine learning · Artificial intelligence · Supervised algorithm · Text mining

M. Botto-Tobar et al. (Eds.): ICCCE 2018, CCIS 959, pp. 98–110, 2019.
https://doi.org/10.1007/978-3-030-12018-4_8

1   Introduction

When someone talks about nanotechnology many definitions come to our head, one of these is when we spoke about tiny robots that make different functions inside the place where they were implanted, but that definitions mention a little part of a large gamma of uses where this science can be used. The "U.S. National Nanotechnology Initiative" (NNI), define the nanotechnology is the science, engineering and technology created in Nano Scale. NNI classified that material between 1 to 100 nm is considered a nano-material. In Fig. 1 the authors showed a size comparison between things.

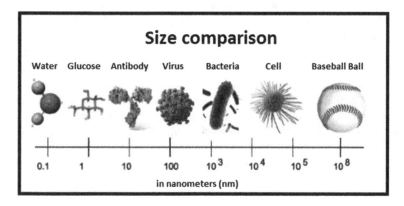

Fig. 1. Size comparison in nanometers

The nanotechnology represents one of the most significant promises of many sci-ences, it is considered as an opportunity to create new solutions that can be very significant through multiple scientific disciplines like the biomedicine [27]. The bio-medicine is a science that applies many natural science principles in the clinical practice through the research of physicopatologic process considered inside the molecular biology, chemistry and physics interactions. The result of combining bio-medicine and nanotechnology give us the nanomedicine that is regarded as science that use nanoparticles and nanomaterials to research new methods that can be used in clinical trials analysis for the physicopatologyc process.

A new approach for the strategic information management obtained by nanome-dicine created a necessity. This improves new data mining methods that helped researchers to get this kind of information. The National Nanomanufacturing Network in 2007 created a new part of nanotechnology for these proposes and they called it nanoinformatic. This science helps to obtain the real vision of what informatics need to do for research about nanotechnology [National Nanomanufacturing Network, 2007]. This branch of nanotechnology involves the development of useful tools, technologies and methods to collect, standardize, integrate, analyze and visualize relevant infor-mation that concerns the nanomedicine, like physicochemical properties, biological, clinical and toxicological effects of the drugs, diseases or nanomaterials. All this information about nanomedicine is inside big repositories of medical trials, but all of this information is messy.

1.1 Nanoinformatics

Nanoinformatics is the science and practice of determining which information is relevant to the nanoscale science and engineering community [25]. And when someone wants to develop and implement effective mechanisms for collecting, validating, storing, sharing, analyzing, modelling, and applying that information, it helps much more.

In [25] shows that this science is necessary for intelligent development and comparative characterization of nanomaterials, for design and use of optimized nanodevices and nanosystems, for development of advanced instrumentation and manufacturing processes, and for assurance of occupational and environmental safety and health. Nanoinformatics also involves the utilization of networked communication tools to launch and support efficient communities of practice. And the most important reason for this work is that this science has to be used because it fosters efficient scientific discovery through data and text mining and machine learning.

When people want to research, this science will allow them to leverage the findings of other efforts in support of their investigations and to improve the impact of their research. In Fig. 2 the authors show the Traditional Scientific Data Lifecycle, and one

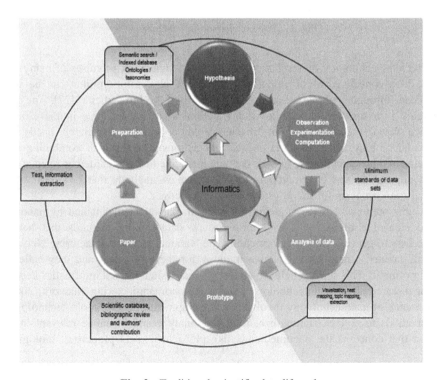

Fig. 2. Traditional scientific data lifecycle

of these steps is the text mining that is used for the extraction of real and important information about the subject that the researcher wants to find out.

1.2 Text Mining

The text mining is used when a researcher wants to process unstructured information, like trials, or some text that is not in databases and help to change it in information that he can use, and, thus, make the information contained in the document accessible to the various data mining using statistical and machine learning algorithms. In text mining, the information can be extracted to derive summaries for the words contained in these documents or to compute summaries for the documents based on the words contained in them. Hence, the researcher can examine words, clusters of words used in documents, etc., or you could analyze documents and determine similarities between them or how they are related to other variables of interest in the data mining project [24].

This article was based on a master thesis [26]. All the process and the pre-process were implemented on a huge base of clinical trials (www.clinicaltrials.gov). On May 08, 2018 the authors downloaded 272,492 clinical trials. In this repository every day many more clinical trials are added.

There are many challenges with the management of databases or repositories of information, such as the automatic classification of these, because there is a problem when a researcher wants to find all of this, because the regular search in a website is based only in the title or the keywords of the trial, but sometimes the trials' authors did not put it in any of this two places, and they talked about it inside the trial. This is the case with the nanomedicine trials, for example in Fig. 3 the authors wrote "nanomedicine" and only two trials were found. As well as knowing where in the world more clinical trials are being done on nanomedicine or related sciences.

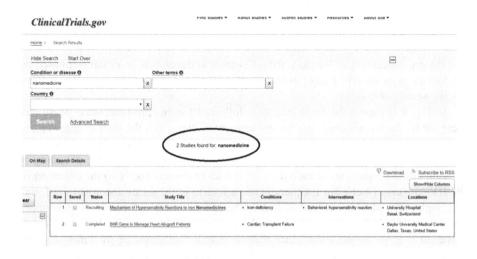

Fig. 3. Searching "nanomedicine" trials

That is the reason why the authors helped to know the percentage of nanomedicine works - nanoparticles, nanodevices, nanomaterials - of one huge repository that contain many types of records such as biomedicine, medicine in general, nanomedicine, uses of medical devices, etc. And this repository is ClinicalTrials.gov that its base is in North America.

The paper is organized as follows: Sect. 2 discusses the methodology and inside, it had the steps that the authors made for obtaining the goal. Section 3 presents Results of the pre-processing method and the process of classification. Section 4 describes the conclusion, and finally, Sect. 5 presents some suggest areas for further investigation.

2   Methodology

The method used in this work was the union of three essential phases that helped this method of text mining that was applied to clinical trial records, the first is the collection of the database for the training of the algorithm and the database for the algorithm test; second is the clinical trials pre-processing to obtain the bag of unigrams (it can be defined as a token extracted from the text) and to transform them into files that the classifying algorithm could read and thus build the model for comparison with the total repository that includes all the clinical trials obtained from the ClinicalTrials.gov page And the third one is already comparing the model with the databases and obtaining the results for the correct discussion of the topic of this work.

2.1   Database and Resources

For the training of the model proceeded to download the article from https://www. clinicaltrials.gov. After that, we proceeded to separate the clinical trials that contained the term "nano" and those that did not.

2.2   Text Pre-processing

For the pre-processing of the data, the software was developed in Visual.Net based on the logistic regression of Lasso, to filter terms, digits and phrases that are not necessary for the search of patterns.

In Fig. 4 is shown the steps that were followed for this pre-processing phase that were 10: (i) the tokenization, (ii) the replacement of digits, (iii) the putting in lowercase letters, (iv) the elimination of stop words, (v) the elimination of textual characteristics, (vi) the obtaining of the frequencies of each term per document, (vii) the obtaining of the sum of the frequencies of each term for the set of documents, (viii) the obtaining of the IDF (Inverse Document Frequency) of each term in the set of documents, (ix & x) and apply two rules that helped to reduce the bag of words to be able to make more precise the classification. In order to do these steps, the programming language Visual Basic 2010 Express was used, since it is an easy-to-use language for functions with words, and contains functions that helped me to separate and replace texts in a simpler and faster way.

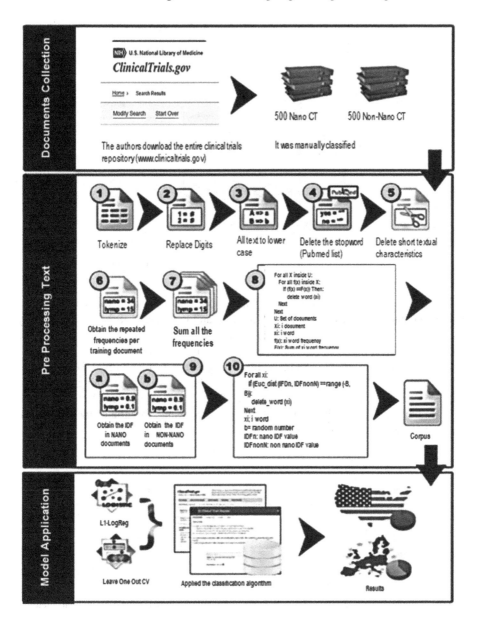

Fig. 4. The procedure of the methodology to be followed

2.3 Software Developed for the Pre-processing

For this phase, is important to know that the authors developed the software on Visual Basic 2010 Express to classify the training base, and used Microsoft Access 2010 for database.

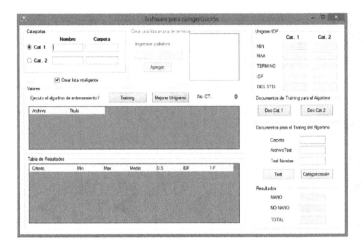

Fig. 5. The interface of the software for pre-processing

In this tool the authors had two possibilities to create the bag of words or unigrams, one is to create the quick list using the 10 steps and the other is if the authors already had a bag of words assigned and they only want to transform the files so that the classifier can read them. In this work, the authors used the first one.

As a first step, the authors had to write in the first box (shown in Fig. 5) the label of each category for the future classification. Next, they pressed the training button and the list began to be created in the row of data found in the part called "Values", which showed the name of the files that are being pre-processing, the title of the record, the date it was published and the number of unigrams found in it (Fig. 6).

Valores

Ejecuto el algoritmo de entrenamiento?   Training   Mejorar Unigrams   No. CT :   0

Archivo	Titulo	Unigrams	Fecha	
NCT00004705.xml	STUDY OF URI...	158	06/23/2005	
NCT00005942.xml	LIPOSOMAL DA...	370	01/22/2013	
NCT00039117.xml	OBLIMERSEN. C...	310	06/03/2013	
NCT00046423.xml	A TRIAL OF ABI-...	168	07/14/2008	

Fig. 6. Result of the revised files, showing their title, number of unigrams and date of publication

Pressing the training button, the first 7 steps were applied, until obtaining the IDF values for the "NANO" category, and a data table was filled. This table is called TABLE OF RESULTS that is showed at Fig. 7.

Tabla de Resultados

Criterio	Min	Max	Media	D.S.	IDF	1-P	^
study	4	16	7.9	3.81	0	0	
uridine	0	4	0.4	1.2	1.7	9	
triphosphate	0	3	0.3	0.9	1.7	9	
utp	0	10	1	3	1.7	9	
aerosol	0	3	0.3	0.9	1.7	9	v

Fig. 7. Table of results, showing the unigrams and the corresponding values to each one

When these steps were done and a bag of words or tokens were created, the software asked to apply the first rule; that is the 8th step in Fig. 4. This process helped to obtain the words that were going to be used for classification. Finally, one last message will appear, informing that category 1 is complete.

The next step was to choose the "NO_NANO" category. In the same way, as in the previous process, the software showed a message when the process has finished with this second category and show the result in the total picture.

To complete the pre-processing the authors had to press the "Improve Unigrams" button. This process is for apply the second rule that was created to improve the bag of words, in this case, corresponds to steps 9 and 10 above.

2.4   Development of the Model

For this phase, the authors used 500 clinical trials:

1. The 250 nanomedicine clinical trials, and,
2. The 250 no nanomedicine clinical trials,

These were chosen manually from the repository of ClinicalTrials.gov. The authors searched about trials with the word "*nano*" and randomly took 250. When the authors read these clinical trials, some of these were about nano devices, but these devices only use "nano" on their names because they were tiny but not nanometric, and because of these error the authors had to read all of them to make sure that they were about nanomedicine.

After the manual classification, all these trials had to be transformed. The authors chose the set of records of clinical training trials with the label "NANO". Then they made it go through a process of transformation, which chose the group of unigrams that are inside each trial and transformed them into an index number and followed by the symbol of two points ":" the IDF value of that term is added to it.

Finally, the authors transformed all the documents in the repository and thus obtain a single document with all the values. And for finished this phase the authors had to do the same procedure with the second category but this time, in the beginning, we put the label of 2, and with that they already differentiate the records of each category. This is recorded in a single file.

2.5   Model Application: Logistic Regression Algorithm

For this phase, the authors used Python 2.7 with the library called LibLinear.

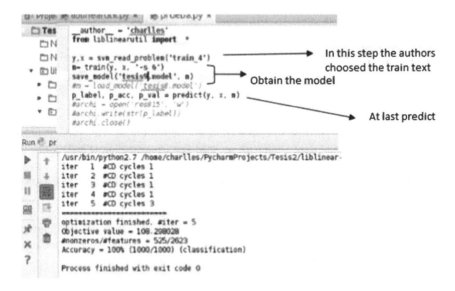

Fig. 8. Python software to create the model for the classification

When the single file is obtained, it was used to create the model for comparison and then classification. Like the Fig. 8 shows in the part of "svm_read_problem" the authors had to put the single file, then it was trained and finally, it was tested.

The next step was to test the model obtained, first it was tested with the training repositories, and these clinical trial records had to be transformed into text files with IDF values. This step helped the authors be sure to use it for the entire repository. The only drawback between these pre-processing is the time it takes to transform these records into text files, which the authors will put as an essential item in future research to find ways to make these transformations faster.

In [26] showed that the model used is the model12, in this master thesis, showed the entire test that the author did.

3   Results

For make this pre-processing and comparison for training and testing the 272,492 clinical trials, the authors used a laptop with Windows 10 with 8 Gb of RAM, Core i7 7th Generation, and for the process the authors used a Virtual Machine with Ubuntu 14.07 LTS with 2 Gb RAM and the same processor that they used on Windows. Table 1 shows the time that the 10 phases and the process of this method took.

Table 1. Total time that the pre-process and process took

Phases	Day	Hours	Minutes
1rst, 2nd & 3rd	2	6	15
4th, 5th & 6th	3	8	26
7th & 8th	0	11	21
9th	1	0	12
10th	0	10	5
Process	0	0	3
Total	7 days 8 h y 32 min		

The time it took to make the model was 26 s after the pre-processing, the time of transforming the two deposits into documents that can be used by the linear regression algorithm was 1 day 18 h, and finally the time to give us the percentages of the classifier varied according to the size of the repository, in this case, it was between 1 min 26 s and 2 min 03 s.

At last, the authors separated the clinical trials in 14 folders, because was more accessible to compare it by 20,000 trials each folder that compare all the 272,492 trials. After obtaining the model to be used for the logistic regression classification, it was used with the entire Clinical Trials Repository of medicine from ClinicalTrials.gov portal, and these were the results (Table 2):

Table 2. Obtained results

	Clinical trials				
	NO NANO	QTY	NANO	QTY	TOTAL
Part 1	91.935%	18387	8.065%	1613	20000
Part 2	91.775%	18355	8.225%	1645	20000
Part 3	90.380%	18076	9.620%	1924	20000
Part 4	90.585%	18116	9.4155	1884	20000
Part 5	90.055%	18011	9.945%	1989	20000
Part 6	90.245%	18049	9.755%	1951	20000
Part 7	90.095%	18019	9.905%	1981	20000
Part 8	89.1205	17824	10.880%	2176	20000
Part 9	88.752%	23371	11.248%	2962	26333
Part 10	86.61%	17299	13.39%	2701	20173
Part 11	85.58%	17116	14.42%	2884	20000
Part 12	85.73%	17146	14.27%	2854	20000
Part 13	85.30%	17061	14.70%	2939	20000
Part 14	84.03%	5030	15.97%	956	5986
TOTAL			11.17%	30,459	272,492

The first 20,000 documents are the older trials, and the last folder had the recent clinical trials. Figure 9 shows the increased of nanomedical clinical trials from older ones to the new ones. In 2015 the researches started to use nanomedicine for many diseases, and the most important of these is cancer. And for now 2018 the Fig. 9 shows that the use of nanomedicine is growing up, the last folder is only the first three months of 2018.

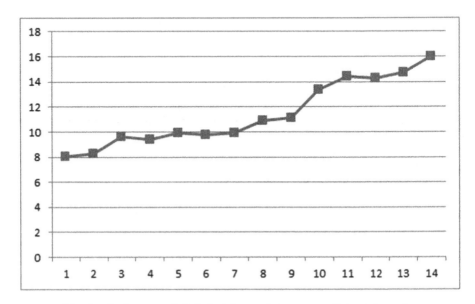

Fig. 9. The increase of clinical trials containing nanomedicine information

4   Conclusion

The authors provided an application developed for this classification and also implement a new method of pre-processing text that is based on 10 steps. The authors used them to classify these clinical trial records and to make this training model easier. Thanks to this method applied in the repository, valuable new records containing nanomedicine and nanotechnology information could be discovered, that with the normal algorithm of search was not discovered.

There were 30,459 clinical trials that are about nanomedicine in this repository that is one of the huge repositories of clinical trials until May 8th, 2018.

It was also possible to extract the potential terms and new patterns in the data of nanomedical areas such as genotoxicity and targeted drug therapy, where certain underlying patterns and trends could lead to inferences that inform future nanomedicine research.

Also in Fig. 9, the authors showed the growth of trials related to nanomedicine, which shows that it is now much easier to find information related to this area, in addition to the use that is being made for the control of diseases.

5 Future Works

For future works with the data obtained in this repository can be used to classify new future categories, such as dividing these records of clinical trials in nanomedicines, nanotoxicity, nanodevices, nanomaterials, physical, biological, chemical properties of nanoparticles, diagnostics, therapies, methods and some categories that have to do with nanotechnology.

Other future work is that this training pre-process model can be applied in other repositories from areas of different sciences, for the detection and correction of documents related to a theme, in the same way as that used in the analysis of related information to a given event of big data with the purpose of getting opinions from a group. In addition, comparisons can be made with other repositories of clinical trials to verify the validity of the algorithm created, checking response times, generated graphs, and search accuracy.

References

1. Apte, C., Weiss, S.: Data mining with decision trees and decision rules. Future Gener. Comput. Syst. **13**, 197–210 (1997)
2. Brücher, H., Gerhard, K., Marc-André, M.: Document Classification Methods for Organizing Explicit Knowledge, Research Group Information Engineering, Institute of Information Systems, University of Bern, Engehaldenstrasse 8, CH - 3012 Bern, Switzerland (2002)
3. Buxton, D.B.: Current status of nanotechnology approaches for cardiovascular disease: a personal perspective. Wiley Interdiscip. Rev. Nanomed. Nanobiotechnol. **1**(2), 149–155 (2009)
4. Apte, C., Damerau, F., Weiss, S.M.: Automated learning of decision rules for text categorization. ACM Trans. Inf. Syst. (TOIS) **12**(3), 233–251 (1994)
5. Chiesa, S., García-Remesal, M., de la Calle, G., de la Iglesia, D., Bankauskaite, V., Maojo, V.: Building an index of nanomedical resources: an automatic approach based on text mining. In: Proceedings of the KES2008, pp. 50–57 (2008)
6. Cios, K., Kacprzyk, J. (Eds.): Medical Data Mining and Knowledge Discovery. Springer, New York (2001)
7. De la Iglesia, D., et al.: Nanoinformatics: new challenges for biomedical informatics at the nano level. Stud. Health Technol. Inform. **150**, 987–991 (2009)
8. De la Iglesia, D., et al.: International efforts in nanoinformatics research applied to nanomedicine. Methods Inf. Med. **50,** 84–95 (2011)
9. De la Iglesia, D., et al.: A machine learning approach to identify clinical trials involving nanodrugs and nanodevices from ClinicalTrials.gov. Plos One **9**(10), e110331 (2013)
10. De la Iglesia, D.: Nanoinformatics knowledge infrastructures: bringing efficient information management to nanomedical research. Comput. Sci. Discov. **6**(1), 014011 (2013). PMC. Web. 17 June 2015

11. Nguyen, D.H.M., Patrick, J.D.: Research and applications: supervised machine learning and active learning in classification of radiology reports. JAMIA **21**(5), 893–901 (2014)
12. Etheridge, M.L., Campbell, S.A., Erdman, A.G., Haynes, C.L., Wolf, S.M., McCullough, J.: The big picture on nanomedicine: the state of investigational and approved nanomedicine products. Nanomedicine **9**(1), 1–14 (2013)
13. EU Framework Project 7. ACTION-Grid. http://www.action-grid.eu
14. Fan, R.E., Chang, K.-W., Hsieh, C.-J., Wang, X.-R., Lin, C.-J.: LIBLINEAR: a library for large linear classification. J. Mach. Learn. Res. **9**, 1871–1874 (2008)
15. Freitas, R.A.: Nanomedicine, Volume IIA: Biocompatibility. Georgetown, Texas: Landes Bioscience (2005). http://www.nanomedicine.com/NMIIA.htm
16. García-Remesal, M., García-Ruiz, A., Pérez-Rey, D., de la Iglesia, D., Maojo, V.: Using nanoinformatics methods for automatically identifying relevant nanotoxicology entities from the literature. Biomed. Res. Int. (2012)
17. Gayathri, K., Marimutha, A.: Multi-class text classification with KNN machine learning techniques **2**(6), 645–647 (2014)
18. Genkin, A., Lewis, D.D., Madigan, D.: Large-scale bayesian logistic regression for text categorization. Technometrics **49**(3), 291–304 (2007)
19. Grulke, C.M., Goldsmith, M.R., Vallero, D.A.: Toward a blended ontology: applying knowledge systems to compare therapeutic and toxicological nanoscale domains. J. Biomed. Biotechnol. (2012)
20. Horev-Azaria, L., Baldi, G., Beno, D., et al.: Predictive toxicology of cobalt ferrite nanoparticles: comparative in-vitro study of different cellular models using methods of knowledge discovery from data. Part. Fibre Toxicol. **10**(1), 32 (2013). https://doi.org/10.1186/1743-8977-10-32
21. Karalis, V., Macheras, P.: Current regulatory approaches of bioequivalence testing. Expert Opin. Drug Metab. Toxicol. **8**, 929–942 (2012)
22. Khan, A., Baharudin, B., Lee, L.H., Khan, K.: A review of machine learning algorithms for text documents classification. J. Adv. Inf. Technol. **1**, 4–20 (2010)
23. Kleiner, R.E., Dumelin, C.E., Liu, D.R.: Small-molecule discovery from DNA encoded chemical libraries. Chem. Soc. Rev. **40**, 5707–5717 (2010)
24. Text Mining (Big Data, Unstructured Data): StatSoft, TIBCA STATICA (2017). http://www.statsoft.com/Textbook/Text-Mining
25. Nanoinformatics group (2011). http://nanoinformatics.org/nanoinformatics/index.php/Nanoinformatics:WhatisNanoinformatics
26. Pérez Espinoza, C.: Uso de técnicas de minería de texto para la identificación de ensayos clínicos en nanomedicina. Thesis (Master thesis), E.T.S. de Ingenieros Informáticos (UPM) (2015)
27. Quirke, V., Gaudilliere, J.-P.: The era of biomedicine: science, medicine and health in Britain and France, ca 1945–1965. In: Quirke, V., Gaudilliere, J.-P. (eds) special issue of Medical History, vol. 52, pp. 441–452 (2008)

Reading Comprehension in University Texts: The Metrics of Lexical Complexity in Corpus Analysis in Spanish

Jenny Ortiz Zambrano$^{(\boxtimes)}$ ⓘ and Eleanor Varela Tapia$^{(\boxtimes)}$ ⓘ

Computer System Engineering Career,
University of Guayaquil, University Campus "Salvador Allende",
Delta Av. and Kennedy Av., Guayaquil, Ecuador
{jenny.ortizz,eleanor.varelat}@ug.edu.es

Abstract. The article focuses on the practical field of the development and implementation of a software application developed for the automatic processing of eight metrics to calculate the lexical complexity in a corpus that contains the transcriptions of university educational videos in Spanish called VYTEDU, prepared by teachers from the University of Guayaquil, Ecuador. The obtained result allowed to demonstrate the different indexes of lexical complexity that the texts have in terms of the comprehensibility of their content. One of the main characteristics of the texts lies in the difference in size and content. It should be noted that although some texts had greater content, the index of lexical complexity was lower than other texts whose content was smaller in size. The diffusion of the software supposes the use of it as a tool to continue researching in the field of Natural Language Processing. The application developed using free software tools facilitated the use of libraries in the field of Natural Language Processing contributing to the analysis of the complexity of text comprehension, making this research a second step to build an automatic simplification tool for text in Spanish in the higher academic field that is proposed as future work, since the first step was the construction of the VYTEDU corpus together with its publication.

Keywords: Reading comprehension · Lexical complexity · Metrics · Free software

1 Introduction

Higher education institutions expect receiving students whose reading comprehension skills have reached an adequate level to be able to face higher education [1]. But this does not happen in reality, even in daily practice we find students who have difficulty not only in reading a text, but also in writing a text, presence of spelling mistakes in the writing of some material, they read but do not understand, anyway, this, therefore, hinders the understanding of the content of the texts [2], and if we add the lexical complexity with which some texts are written, it becomes a barrier in its comprehensibility and therefore in learning, since it is indisputable that texts are a source of knowledge [1].

The readability is one of the required elements so that the content of the information can be understood in a simple and clear way, while the relative difficulty that appears

© Springer Nature Switzerland AG 2019
M. Botto-Tobar et al. (Eds.): ICCCE 2018, CCIS 959, pp. 111–123, 2019.
https://doi.org/10.1007/978-3-030-12018-4_9

when deciphering the written words would be a cause for the readers of any level not to understand the content of information [3], knowing that comprehension consists in understanding the meaning of content presented in a text [4].

There are two factors that hinder the comprehension of reading in a text: the first is not knowing the lexicon[1], that is, the words, and therefore their definition; success or failure of the reader's understanding of a text will depend on knowledge or ignorance of the words that compose it, creating a barrier in the second language students in this case of Spanish, people who have some kind of special capacity as Asperger, Down syndrome, Autism or also in people with low literacy.

The second factor is the difficulty in recognizing syntactic structures, that is, the order in which words should appear in sentences or phrases to avoid ambiguities when making an expression [4].

We present the results of a recent work carried out in the CEATIC[2] in September 2017, where eight measures were applied to calculate the lexical complexity in the VYTEDU[3] corpus; the metrics that were considered were those defined by the authors: Anula (2008) [5], Saggion (2015) [6], and Spaulding (1956) [7].

The objective of this research is to analyze the lexical complexity contained in the texts of the corpus.

Section 2 presents the related works where the lexical complexity metrics have been applied, as well as where the metrics have been applied in the text simplification systems even for the simplification systems proposed for Spanish.

Section 3 shows the Materials and methods that have been applied, as well as an explanation in detail of each of the text complexity metrics proposed by different authors.

In Sect. 4, the results and the discussion are presented through an analysis of the data obtained from the application of the lexical complexity metrics in the VYTEDU corpus and university texts.

In the last section we present the conclusions and future works that can be undertaken from this research work.

Finally, we thank the researchers from University of Jaén who contributed to this research.

2   Related Work

In the researched documents, literature has been found in which lexical readability metrics are implemented to evaluate complexity with the many texts written. These measures are mostly implemented by the automatic text simplification systems but have not yet been implemented in the educational field.

---

[1] Lexicon – According to the dictionary of the Royal Academy of the Spanish Language, its meaning is the "set of words of a language, or those that belong to the use of a region". Official website available at http://dle.rae.es/?id=ND3Rym3.

[2] CEATIC: Center for Advanced Studies of the University of Jaén (Jaén-España). (by its initials in Spanish).

[3] VYTEDU: Videos and Transcripts in the Educational field. (by its initials in Spanish).

According to Saggion (2015) the way in which the texts are written can be a difficulty, resulting for many people being a barrier, which can affect many users such as: non-native speakers, people with little literacy level, people with cognitive specials abilities [6].

The metrics of the lexical complexity were also calculated in the implementation of a simplification system of texts in Spanish called Simplext that evaluated the complexity with the objective of creating accessible texts.

In many researches works, metrics have been used to evaluate the systems for automatic simplification of texts for Spanish, these systems seek the comprehensibility of the texts.

Seven measures of lexical readability (except measure 8 - ARI) were automatically calculated in a system of evaluation related to systems of simplification of texts in Spanish, tested in a corpus of original news texts and their manual simplifications oriented to people with special cognitive abilities [8], we have taken as reference base for our purpose in this investigation, the calculation of the lexical complexity of university texts in Spanish in the VYTEDU corpus, to determine the complication that could result in students reading non-readable texts.

Recent studies show that lexical readability metrics have been applied to demonstrate the most important features to determine the recommended age for reading children's texts, where the work applies to twelve of the metrics most commonly used to calculate lexical and syntactic readability, which are the formulas of Anula (2008), Spaulding (1956) and Saggion (2015), obtaining as a result that the factors of lexical or syntactic complexity in any case do not determine the recommended reading but the key factor is in the use of certain vocabulary [9].

3   Materials and Methods

3.1   Characteristics of Materials

All text files contained in VYTEDU were considered. This corpus is made up of 55 videos along with their respective transcripts in the higher academic field and they correspond to different subjects dictated by the teachers, these texts were recorded during the class day, within the classrooms of the University of Guayaquil, Ecuador.

One of the main characteristics of the texts lies in the difference in size and content. It should be noted that although some texts had greater content, the index of lexical complexity was lower than other texts whose content was smaller in size.

3.2   Method

They are a total of 8 metrics that were considered and implemented in the analysis of the texts of the corpus, the metrics proposed by Anula (2008) to calculate the lexical complexity, are the ones shown below (Table 1):

$$LC = (LDI + ILFW)/2 \tag{1}$$

$$ILFW = N(lfw)/N(cw) * 100 \tag{2}$$

$$LDI = N(dcw)/N(s) \tag{3}$$

Table 1. Basic definitions for the calculation of the complexity measure.

Component	Detail
LDI	Index of lexical distribution
ILFW	Index of low frequency words
N(dcw)	Number of different content words
N(cw)	Number of total content words
N(s)	Number of sentences in the text
N(lfw)	Number of low frequency words

The measure proposed by Spaulding (1956) was also taken in consideration: SSR-Spaulding Spanish Readability, the implementation of this formula allows to obtain in an exact way the difficulty of reading a material, this formula has been implemented in several research works to obtain the levels of reading difficulty in school textbooks [7].

$$SSR = 1.609N(w)/N(s) + 331.8\,N(rw)/N(w) + 22.0 \tag{4}$$

where, N(w): number of words in the text.

Other measures also proposed by Anula (2008) were implemented to calculate the Sentence Complexity Index, as a measure of the complexity of sentences in literary texts [5], they are:

$$SCI = (ASL + CS)/2 \tag{5}$$

$$ASL = N(w)/N(s) \tag{6}$$

$$CS = N(cs)/N(s) \tag{7}$$

where, N(cs): number of complex sentences.

One of the indexes most used for its ease of calculation is the Automated Readability Index, better known as the ARI (Automated Readability Index) for its acronym in English. This index measures the difficulty of a text based on the average number of characters (letters and numbers) per word and the average number of words per sentence, the formula indicates the following:

$$4.71 * num\_characters/num\_words + 0.5 * num\_words/num\_sentences - 21.43 \tag{8}$$

It refers to a readability test designed to measure the comprehensibility of a text, that is, how easy it is to understand the text [6, 10]. The greater the value of this index, the more difficult the text presents. The result of this formula is a number that approaches the level of the reader's necessary degree to understand the text.

To carry out this task, first, the plain text .txt files containing the transcripts of the VYTEDU videos were re-recorded using the UTF-8[4] format.

A function was created to take as an input a list of tokens and generate a list of sentences. For this, we carried out the treatment of each text through the following steps:

1. The text of the file read was passed to this function as input and the result was the generation of a list of tokens, each token corresponded to a term (word, number or punctuation mark). Abbreviations such as US, U.S.A, among others, words with intermediate hyphens, currencies and percentages were allowed, e.g.: $ 12.40, 35%, 36.3 €, ellipsis "…", more than two spaces, also the symbols [.,; ""? (): - _`'] were considered isolated tokens, and once the tokens were extracted from the text they were converted to lowercase.

2. Then we group the obtained tokens by sentences, for this the end of sentence markers were specified.

3. We proceeded to the elimination of words of low semantic content, those words are also known as empty words [11], these are words that have no meaning or as they are also called: stop words (in English). To achieve that, it was enough to go through the tokens and eliminate those terms that appear in a dictionary of empty words, NLTK incorporates one of these dictionaries for Spanish.

4. Currently, NLTK does not have a POS-tagger[5]. Commonly called POS Tagging, it is a labeling of the words of a text according to its grammatical category, but we can use the NLP group of Stanford University; the tagger[6] was downloaded from Stanford University and placed on the same route where the notebook is located, proceeding to unzip it [12, 13].

Later, each token was converted into a tuple, the same one that was made up of the token and the POS (Part-Of-Speech tagger that specifies if the token is a noun, verb, pronoun, preposition, adverb, conjunction, participle and article).

Finally, we proceeded to filter to stay alone with adjectives, verbs and nouns. With all this, the following structures were obtained:

- The list of sentences, in which each sentence is a list of tokens.
- List of words but without empty words.
- List of words but associating the POS of each word.
- List of words keeping adjectives, verbs and nouns.

---

[4] UTF-8: (8-bit Unicode Transformation Format). According to Yergeau (2003) "it is a transformation format of ISO 10646".

[5] POS-tagger – Part-Of-Speech tagger, also known as POS Tagging, Mesa (2016).

[6] TAGGER of Stanford University, available at https://nlp.stanford.edu/software/stanford-postagger-full-2017-06-09.zip.

Low-frequency words were calculated, then the number of words with different content, the number of sentences, the total number of total content words and the index of low frequency words were calculated. The data previously obtained allowed us to calculate the Index of Lexical Distribution - LDI.

4   Results and Discussion

4.1   Results

Finally, the LC - Lexical Complexity was obtained, whose values came from the calculations previously made (see Fig. 1). As a result of the application of the formulas to obtain the index of the lexical complexity in each university text, the following were obtained: the number of low frequency words, the number of different words and the number of sentences, which in turn allowed obtaining the indexes of the lexical distribution, index of words of low frequency and the lexical complexity of the text (see Fig. 1).

```
Trabajando en:  Video-01-Licenciatura en sistema de informacion.txt ........

LEXICAL COMPLEXITY INDEX:
Number of low frequency words (N_lfw):  491

Number of distinct content words (N_dcw) = 281
Number os sentences (N_s):  46

Number of total content words (N_cw):  491

Lexical Distribution Index (LDI) = 6.108695652173913
Index Low Frequency Words (ILFW) = 0.7462006079027356
Lexical Complexity (LC) = 3.427448130038324
```

Fig. 1. Execution of the application for the calculation of the metrics of the lexical complexity in the VYTEDU corpus.

The basic results have been achieved that will allow us to complement the analysis of the formulas proposed in Sect. 3.

Some statistical formulas were also implemented in the developed code that helped to complement the analysis of the lexical complexity of the texts, such as: minimum value, maximum value, median and quartiles. After processing the VYTEDU corpus files (see Fig. 2). As can be seen the most relevant data is shown after processing each text of the corpus, which will show us the legibility of the corpus texts, obtained according to the proposed formula, it can be observed that both the number of low frequency words such as the index of low frequency words are within normal values, do not exceed the limit, that is, these are those that can not be found in the list of the 1500 most common Spanish words provided by Spaulding (1956) [6], which means that the lexicon used by two teachers facilitates learning in students.

	N_charac	N_w	N_dcw	N_cw	N_lfw	N_rw	N_s	N_cs	LDI	ILFW	LC
count	55.000000	55.00000	55.000000	55.000000	55.000000	55.000000	55.000000	55.000000	55.000000	55.000000	55.000000
mean	6299.290909	1369.80000	338.200000	614.309091	363.836364	363.836364	33.854545	14.872727	12.384541	0.592512	6.488526
std	2162.429427	507.50911	91.039552	214.543863	134.723415	134.723415	15.152824	7.542606	6.417844	0.093634	3.184586
min	2598.000000	541.00000	102.000000	246.000000	131.000000	131.000000	6.000000	2.000000	4.431818	0.391892	2.568850
25%	4823.000000	992.00000	270.000000	466.000000	272.500000	272.500000	21.000000	10.000000	7.614510	0.525862	4.131245
50%	6168.000000	1282.00000	347.000000	593.000000	358.000000	358.000000	36.000000	14.000000	10.909091	0.588764	5.791424
75%	7203.500000	1506.00000	393.000000	722.500000	431.000000	431.000000	45.500000	19.000000	16.219608	0.667145	8.343859
max	13034.000000	2918.00000	527.000000	1218.000000	723.000000	723.000000	64.000000	39.000000	30.000000	0.786070	15.274576

Fig. 2. Implementation of statistical formulas in the results from the Lexical Complexity in the archives of the VYTEDU corpus.

It should be noted that according to the analysis of the data, the LC (Lexical Complexity) in some texts is high, which means that the content becomes difficult in some cases, this is also due to the number of rare words that the teachers are using when they teach their classes. With the above data, the SSR could already be calculated (see Fig. 3).

	N_w	N_rw	N_s	SSR
count	55.00000	55.000000	55.000000	55.000000
mean	1369.80000	363.836364	33.854545	194.772047
std	507.50911	134.723415	15.152824	43.401093
min	541.00000	131.000000	6.000000	128.673246
25%	992.00000	272.500000	21.000000	165.236479
50%	1282.00000	358.000000	36.000000	184.023145
75%	1506.00000	431.000000	45.500000	209.263559
max	2918.00000	723.000000	64.000000	332.320273

Fig. 3. Calculation of the SSR in the texts of the VYTEDU corpus.

The result obtained when classifying the SSR - Spoulding Spanish Readability in the texts of the corpus is the following: the mean is considered in the value of 184 what it means according to the table of reference values proposed (120 - and above) [7], the texts present an exceptional difficulty of being read the texts written in Spanish. 25% of the texts have a value of 165, which according to the table of values are also within the range of exceptional difficulty, while 75% and the rest are above the values described previously. The university texts used in this analysis are within the level of excessive difficulty, their content can not be easily read without having to resort to mental skills exercises and implementation of types of concentration to understand their content.

The SCI proposed by Anula (2008) as a measure of the complexity of sentences in a literary text, next, the ASL (Average Sentence Length) and the CS (Complex Sentence) were calculated, finally obtaining the SCI (Sentence Complexity Index).

Punctuation marks (PUNCT) refers to the average number of punctuation marks per text. This can be obtained with a POS and counting the frequency of the PUNCT label (with Freeling, for example). The punctuation marks directly influence the clarity and comprehension of the content of the text contributing to its correct interpretation [14].

After implementing the statistical measures in the results obtained from the calculation of the metrics (see Fig. 4).

	LC	SSR	ASL	CS	SCI	ARI	PM
count	55.000000	55.000000	55.000000	55.000000	55.000000	55.000000	55.000000
mean	6.488526	194.772047	51.852806	0.516384	26.184595	26.341149	111.963636
std	3.184586	43.401093	32.381573	0.260293	16.296772	15.090235	55.711879
min	2.568850	128.673246	13.886364	0.041667	6.988636	8.377110	26.000000
25%	4.131245	165.236479	27.214015	0.299934	13.804924	15.433365	74.500000
50%	5.791424	184.023145	39.288889	0.500000	19.966667	20.507724	102.000000
75%	8.343859	209.263559	69.937255	0.710084	35.345098	33.469021	138.500000
max	15.274576	332.320273	132.666667	1.000000	66.750000	65.333187	344.000000

Fig. 4. Implementation of the statistical formulas in the results of the metrics executed in the VYTEDU corpus.

It can be seen that the average lexical complexity of the corpus obtained is 6.48, the minimum value is 2.6 and the maximum value is 15.27 according to the data (see Fig. 4).

For the analysis of the data obtained from the application of the lexical complexity metrics in the texts of the university videos those texts were chosen taking into account the number of words and their respective result of the lexical complexity - LC, it is considered that not necessarily the texts that are composed of more words are those that have higher LC index, for this we have considered as an example the texts Video-17 and Video-10. (see Fig. 5).

	N_charac	N_w	N_dcw	N_cw	N_lfw	N_rw	N_s	N_cs	LDI	ILFW	LC
Video-01	6529.0	1510.0	281.0	658.0	491.0	491.0	46.0	14.0	6.108696	0.746201	3.427448
Video-10	13034.0	2918.0	516.0	1218.0	723.0	723.0	35.0	19.0	14.742857	0.593596	7.668227
Video-17	2598.0	541.0	198.0	246.0	140.0	140.0	16.0	4.0	12.375000	0.569106	6.472053
Video-24	2966.0	611.0	195.0	306.0	216.0	216.0	44.0	4.0	4.431818	0.705882	2.568850
Video-55	3197.0	768.0	180.0	295.0	162.0	162.0	6.0	6.0	30.000000	0.549153	15.274576

Fig. 5. Calculation of the Lexical Complexity - LC.

The text Video-17 has a quantity of 541 words and the text Video-10 has a total of 2918 words corresponding to the minimum and maximum value of words respectively according to the statistical data presented in Fig. 5. The values of the measure of LC are 6.47 and 7.668 respectively, that is, with a fairly short difference; if we compare it with the number of words in the Video-55 text that we have taken as reference because according to Fig. 5 it is the one with the highest value of LC, it is composed of 768 words and an LC of 15,274 is located like the one of greater LC of all the corpus, that is, to say a text of great complexity.

It is worth mentioning that there are texts such as Video-24 which is composed of 611 words, just a little above the total number of words in the Video-17 text, but it has an LC of 2.56, which is much lower than the LC of the Video-17 text. it is 6.47, which can be concluded as a text of easy comprehensibility. Regarding to the SSR measure, in the values presented in Fig. 5, if we take these texts as a sample, we would have the data presented for the SSR (see Fig. 6).

	N_charac	N_w	N_dcw	N_cw	N_lfw	N_rw	N_s	N_cs	LDI	ILFW	LC	SSR
Video-01	6529.0	1510.0	281.0	658.0	491.0	491.0	46.0	14.0	6.108696	0.746201	3.427448	182.707108
Video-10	13034.0	2918.0	516.0	1218.0	723.0	723.0	35.0	19.0	14.742857	0.593596	7.668227	238.355526
Video-17	2598.0	541.0	198.0	246.0	140.0	140.0	16.0	4.0	12.375000	0.569106	6.472053	162.267529
Video-55	3197.0	768.0	180.0	295.0	162.0	162.0	6.0	6.0	30.000000	0.549153	15.274576	297.941062
Video-24	2966.0	611.0	195.0	306.0	216.0	216.0	44.0	4.0	4.431818	0.705882	2.568850	161.640704

Fig. 6. Calculation of the Spaulding Spanish Readability - SSR.

The SSR is related to the number of words, that is why we will analyze the texts of Fig. 5. We can observe according to the data presented in Fig. 6, we see that the text Video-01 has a total of 1510 words and an SSR of 182,707, while the Video-55 text has a much smaller number of words and has an SSR of 297,941. Also, the text Video-24 has a total of 611 words, that is, at the moment it is the smallest of the texts of this analysis of the SSR presenting an SSR of 161.64. The text Video-10 has an SSR of 238.35 when its total of words is 2918, that is to say a total of words much greater to those presented in the previous texts and its SSR did not surpass the calculated of the text Video-55.

Regarding the SCI analysis of the texts of the corpus, we have taken a sample of texts, observing a very high sentence complexity index; for this, the columns of the number of words, number of sentences, number of complex sentences and the SCI have been considered (see Fig. 7). The text Video-24 contains 611 words and has an SCI of 6.98 while the text Video-55 has 768 words and an SCI totally superior to the previous one being this one of 56.45; text Video-46 is slightly larger in number of words than text Video-55 and its SCI is 66.7, when analyzing the text Video-07, this contrasts the previous ones since the SCI is 11.96.

	N_w	N_s	N_cs	SCI
Video-24	611.0	44.0	4.0	6.988636
Video-38	1119.0	10.0	10.0	56.450000
Video-55	768.0	6.0	6.0	64.500000
Video-48	796.0	6.0	5.0	66.750000
Video-07	1502.0	64.0	30.0	11.968750

Fig. 7. Calculation of the Sentence Complexity Index - SCI.

In the calculation of the ARI made in VYTEDU it can be seen that there is an average of 26.34 where the minimum value calculated is 8.37, which means that it is an easy to read text, while the maximum value calculated is 65.33, this being a text difficult to understand because of the high value obtained (see Fig. 8).

	ARI
count	55.000000
mean	26.341149
std	15.090235
min	8.377110
25%	15.433365
50%	20.507724
75%	33.469021
max	65.333187

Fig. 8. Calculation of the ARI - Automated Readability Index.

The 25% of the texts of the corpus have an ARI lower than 15.43 which is easily accessible, another 25% has an ARI that is between 15.43 and 20.50 which means that it is slightly complex, another 25% is between 20.50 and 33.46, that is, 50% of the texts of the corpus present a moderately complex index of difficulty, while the last 25% have a very complex percentage of comprehension difficulty since it is above 33.46.

The calculations were obtained for Punctuation Marks (PM) (see Fig. 9) where 25% of the texts have a number of punctuation marks lower than 74, another 25% is in the range of 74.50 to 102, while 25% is between 102 to 138 and the last 25% of the texts of VYTEDU have an amount greater than 138.50 with the maximum number of 344 punctuation marks in the content of the text.

	PM
count	55.000000
mean	111.963636
std	55.711879
min	26.000000
25%	74.500000
50%	102.000000
75%	138.500000
max	344.000000

Fig. 9. Statistics obtained from the PM - Punctuation Marks.

According to the results, it can be seen that there are texts that have a very large number of words and a smaller number of punctuation marks compared to others, such as the text Video-07 that has 1502 words and has a PM of 99, while the text Video-01 has 1510 words and a PM of 170, that is, with a slightly higher number of words and a much higher PM. Another case is the text Video-39 with a number of words 2275 and a MW of 91 showing a greater difference in number of words and a much lower MP compared to the text Video-07.

Another case that can be seen is the text Video-45 that contains a number of words of 2417 and a PM of 344, compared to the text Video-10 with a total of 2918 words and a PM of 215, that is to say it presents a radical difference in both the number of words and punctuation marks.

4.2 Discutions

Our research work is aimed at the evaluation of lexical complexity in university texts in Spanish of the VYTEDU corpus, while Saggion et al. took a corpus of 200 news texts from different sections, in both researches works 8 metrics of lexical readability (presented by this research) were applied. Saggion et al. presented the first system of simplification of texts for Spanish to "evaluate the level of reading difficulty of the texts produced by the human being" [6], where comparing with the results of manual simplification, there is a margin that is between a 30% to 40% difference of the values provided from the calculation of the metrics versus the manual simplification performed.

One important aspect must be considered, Saggion et al. propose that these indexes can be used in automatic evaluation in systems of simplification of texts in Spanish to evaluate the complexity of texts, so our research work is based on this premise, which has allowed us to calculate the complexity of the texts and be able to obtain the result of the analysis of these, allowing us to determine the lexical complexity with which the subject is taught by university professors, determining the level of difficulty that is presented to university students in terms of the comprehensibility of their content.

It should be noted that the legibility measures applied by Saggion et al. were also applied in a recent research paper by Lopez et al., the same ones that base their research on the metrics most commonly used to calculate lexical and syntactic readability; in this work twelve measures were applied in a corpus of 300 texts of readings in Spanish addressed to elementary school students, obtaining as a result the determination of the recommended reading age for a text.

These results help us to determine that some of the texts hinder students' reading comprehension, creating a barrier especially in those students with special cognitive abilities what Saggion et al. want to show is that the way in which some texts are written turns out to be a barrier in people.

5 Conclusions and Future Work

It is very significant to end our article presenting the conclusions of the most relevant data that were obtained, as well as the future works that will be developed from it.

The creation of the VYTEDU corpus is a collection of academic videos in the university environment, it is a contribution to continue advancing in the studies in the field of text simplification in Spanish, according to research in the educational field, no proposals have yet been presented.

The analysis of the lexical complexity was carried out in the texts of the VYTEDU corpus. The research work was empirical, based on a corpus of transcribed texts of their respective academic videos. The building of the code through open source tools was necessary for the automated execution of the lexical complexity metrics in the texts of the VYTEDU corpus.

The results obtained show that having a corpus of university texts has allowed us to carry out an analysis in terms of the comprehensibility of its content, which we believe is a great contribution for the scientific community to continue advancing in the study of techniques that help break down the barriers of the difficulty of understanding that originates from the lexical complexity of the content of the texts.

During the analysis we observed that in several of the texts with less content, the complexity index was superior to others that were of greater content and the same for the different measures executed in the VYTEDU corpus. The results show that you have to be very precise in the way you report, as this can cause a learning difficulty.

The application developed using free software tools facilitated the use of libraries in the field of Natural Language Processing contributing to the analysis of the complexity of text comprehension, making this research a second step to build an automatic simplification tool for text in Spanish in the higher academic field that is proposed as future work, since the first step was the construction of the VYTEDU corpus together with its publication.

For future research, the evaluation of the results of the implementation of the metrics in university academic texts can also be extended to analyze the complexity index of academic texts at all educational levels, since the input of this research work consists of contributing to education through the implementation of technological tools that facilitate learning.

Acknowledgments. Our gratitude to the contribution that PhD Alfonso Ureña, director of the PhD program in Information and Communication Technologies of the UJA (University of Jaén) and PhD Arturo Montejo - Director of this research project gave us, and also our thanks to MSc. Rocío Anguita from the University of Granada for her contribution in the development and statistical application of this material.

References

1. Neira Martínez, A.C., Reyes Reyes, F.T., Riffo Ocares, B.E.: Academic experience and reading comprehension strategies in first-year university students. Lit. Linguist. **31**, 221–244 (2015)
2. https://www.laprensa.com.ni/2014/07/03/nacionales/201526-bachilleres-no-leen-ni-escriben-bien. Accessed 5 April 2018
3. Blanco, A., Gutiérrez, C.: Readability of health web pages for patients and readers of the general population. Span. Mag. Publ. Health **76**(4), 321–331 (2002)
4. Raúl Ordoññez, M.: https://revistas.ulima.edu.pe/index.php/Persona/article/view/691/665
5. Anula, A.: Readings adapted to the teaching of Spanish as L2: linguistic variables for determining the level of readability. The evaluation in learning and teaching Spanish as L2, pp. 162–170 (2008)

6. Saggion, H., Štajner, S., Bott, S., Mille, S., Rello, L., Drndarevic, B.: Making it simplext: implementation and evaluation of a text simplification system for spanish. ACM Trans. Accessible Comput. (TACCESS) **6**(4), 14 (2015)
7. Spaulding, S.: A Spanish readability formula. Mod. Lang. J. **40**(8), 433–441 (1956)
8. Štajner, S., Saggion, H.: Readability indices for automatic evaluation of text simplification systems: a feasibility study for spanish. In: Proceedings of the Sixth International Joint Conference on Natural Language Processing, pp. 374–382 (2013)
9. López-Anguita, R., Montejo-Ráez, A., Martínez-Santiago, F.J., Díaz-Galiano, M.C.: Legibility of the text, complexity metrics and the importance of words. Nat. Lang. Process. **61**, 101–108 (2018)
10. Senter, R.J., Smith, E.A.: Automated readability index. Cincinnati Univ. OH (1967)
11. Rodríguez, S.: Extraction of information from emails using natural language processing techniques (2017)
12. Mesa, J.: Processing of natural language and its application in hotel services (2016)
13. Orquín, A., Rodríguez, K., Amable, A., Martín, R., Echarte, Á., Morera, D.C.: System for the pre-processing of texts for Natural Language Processing (2009)
14. De Jesús Torres, J.A.: Design of an educational software for the learning of language and literature in the punctuation marks of the first-year students of general unified baccalaureate morning section, parallel F of the technical institute superior technical center DM Quito, period 2016 (Bachelor's thesis, Quito: UCE). http://www.dspace.uce.edu.ec/handle/25000/11181

Political-Electoral Marketing and Influencing Factors in Student Representatives' Elections Under a Fuzzy Logic Approach

Lorenzo Cevallos-Torres[1(✉)], Miguel Botto-Tobar[1,2],
Jessica Yepez-Holguín[1], Jenny Ortiz-Zambrano[1],
and Nelly Valencia-Martínez[1,2]

[1] Facultad de Ciencias Matemáticas y Físicas - Carrera de Ingeniería en Sistemas
Computacionales, Universidad de Guayaquil, Guayaquil, Ecuador
{lorenzo.cevallost,miguel.bottot,jessica.yepezh,
jenny.ortizz,nelly.valenciam}@ug.edu.ec
[2] Eindhoven University of Technology, Eindhoven, The Netherlands
m.a.botto.tobar@tue.nl

Abstract. This study aimed to determine the causal factors, under uncertainty, related to the decisions taken by students in the University of Guayaquil as voters; at the time of electing a candidate as a student representative; similarly, how effective are electoral marketing strategies applied by parties and student groups for vote-catching. We proposed a methodology based on Fuzzy Logic techniques and cognitive maps to create causality models relying on expert criteria. Being these models useful for decision making, as well as analysis of hypothetical scenarios based on the underlying concept structures that have the most significant causal weight related to the effectiveness of electoral marketing strategies.

Keywords: Fuzzy cognitive maps · Political marketing · Decision making ·
Fuzzy logic · Scenario analyses · Marketing strategy

1 Introduction

Political-electoral marketing has been represented as a fundamental tool for research, planning, and dissemination of strategic actions to develop an electoral campaign, building communicational models, image and a congruent electoral discourse offering solutions to the voter problems. However, political activities and electoral campaigns are processes involved in a wide range of uncertainty where there are factors that can greatly influence the effectiveness of decision making in marketing strategies [2, 8, 18, 28].

The beginnings of political marketing date back to the 50 s in the USA, when General Dwight Eisenhower as presidential candidate requested the services of an advertising agency [22, 26] to advance his television campaign, being the first one to do it. Consequently, it was in this country, where through the communication media, the political marketing started to develop itself progressively and permanently. From this perspective, the candidate ideas and proposals can be distributed with a general

© Springer Nature Switzerland AG 2019
M. Botto-Tobar et al. (Eds.): ICCCE 2018, CCIS 959, pp. 124–138, 2019.
https://doi.org/10.1007/978-3-030-12018-4_10

need of the society, showing the appropriate actions that can be taken into account when finding one or several solutions, in such a way that it achieves the voter's attention [15, 30].

1.1 Political Marketing

According to [30]: political marketing is indispensable for the development of presidential campaigns because it creates new ways to convey messages and ideas and also offers the opportunity to identify the masses, creating the desired reality through their strategies, and thus, approaching to the vote-catching as the main purpose.

For a long time, it has been ensured that one of the most important variables to explain citizens orientation at the time of giving their vote is the partisan identity. On the other hand, political publicity as a technique for voter convincing, and leading to the vote-catching [7, 9, 27, 34].

Rivera Costales in [9] carried out a study focused on Ecuadorian elections in 2006 where Rafael Correa Delgado won as President, hence one of the central points of the victory in this election was an excellent electoral marketing strategy by using social networks and the Internet, and moreover, a relatively youthful fresh profile with new ideas. Mailing [16] was the highlighted technique; it was used to send emails offering the message to all potential voters. The use of new technological strategies for communication and information applied to market, was an innovation in Ecuadorian politics since it allowed to know the candidate profile by voters [21, 39, 40].

1.2 Electoral Marketing

The electoral marketing is part of the politician activity, and as it explains in [1], it refers to a solid electoral campaign, which is in short-term contextualized in a space and a specific time. It is confined to the pre-election stage (for example, three months before the voting date). Hence the politician refers to a continuing action by political parties, to consolidate their ideological stance in front of their voters and the society in which it has or might have a direct impact [13, 37].

Political sciences are firmly based on vague and uncertain affirmations [23]. For the analysis of uncertainty causalities and effects related to electoral marketing, "it is assumed that individual behaviors are determined by their social environment based on elements characteristics such as family life, work or community, and they have an impact on the voting decision" [11, 29, 31, 35].

University of Guayaquil (UG) considered as the largest university in the student population in Ecuador. It has strong political roots and a great sense of democracy empowerment by its students [3], hence, it seeks to motivate its students politically to attend the elections for any student representatives; this process leads students to acquire a fundamental role to understand the political interaction existing inside UG, [14]. However, the political logic shows the opposite every time it refuses by a critical thought and gives relevance to subjet standardization; which reflects in the processes developed by this institution presenting gaps that limit the political formation of its students, and therefore, it reveals that they have a limited vision in terms of democratic participation, causing an uncertainty environment at the time of electing their representatives [4, 6] (Fig. 1).

The goal of this research is to establish the uncertainty factors influencing the students' electoral decisions and to determine whether the application of diffuse cognitive maps, will help optimal decision-making for the development of electoral marketing strategies, in the elections of student representatives in the University of Guayaquil [24].

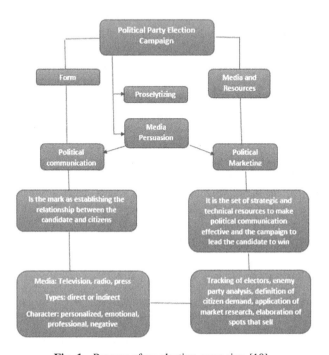

Fig. 1. Process of an election campaign [10].

The paper is organized as follows: Sect. 2 discusses Fuzzy Logic. Section 3 presents Fuzzy Cognitive Maps. Section 4 describes the Mental Modeler tool. Section 5 presents the results obtained, and finally, Sect. 6 presents our conclusions and suggest areas for further investigation.

2   Fuzzy Sets and Fuzzy Logic Systems

The need to model real-world phenomena, which are inherently vague and ambiguous. It makes use of modern mathematical tools, to efficiently process information. For which the use of models based on fuzzy logic allows using concepts related to reality following patterns of behavior similar to human thought, in such a way that will enable us to simulate the presence of these factors, being of great use as support for decision making in politician strategies [24].

In [42] mentioned that in fuzzy logic each uncertainty value would represent a continuous value belonging to a diffuse set defined by the interval of [0, 1]; where 0 represents the total ignorance of any trait, whereas 1 the full knowledge of it. The values located in this range are translated into the uncertainty degree that it has of the feature, thus the values that tend to 0 representing a higher uncertainty degree while those that are typical to 1 a greater certainty degree. Fuzzy logic is generally based on fuzzy rules so that they allow representing the knowledge in the form of a relationship between variables that are used, with the purpose of having a precise and clear result from vague and imprecise information [36].

2.1 Membership Functions

In [41] indicated that typical membership functions such as the triangular, trapezoidal and Gaussian (see Fig. 2). The membership function in a fuzzy set takes all the real values in the interval [0, 1]. Therefore, it assigns a membership degree to a particular set of elements called fuzzy-joint memberships. They will be used in MATLAB's fuzzy Inference system (FIS) [12, 19, 20].

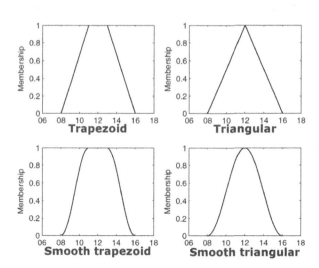

Fig. 2. Membership functions.

A fuzzy inference system (FIS) is a way of representing inaccurate knowledge and data in a similar way as it is done by human thought [41]. A FIS defines a non-linear correspondence between one or more input variables and one output variable. It provides a basis for which to make decisions or define patterns. The FIS development stages are shown in Fig. 3 and they are explained below [38].

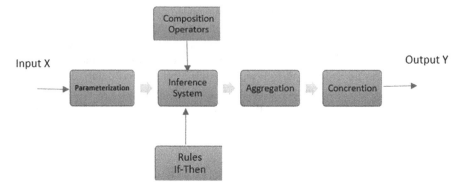

Fig. 3. Fuzzy inference system.

2.2   Causal Weights

For the evaluation of causal weights, we will use Matlab and its tool of fuzzy inference under Mamdani method. For this, we must be clear about which concepts are considered in the electoral political marketing and what causal relationships are to model the system.

Figure 4 shows the linguistic variables and their corresponding membership functions, we used trimmf function for each variable.

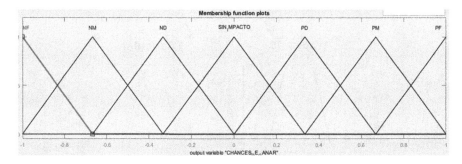

Fig. 4. Variable scheme "Chances to win".

To determine the causal weights between concepts, we support on the expert criteria in student political context in the University of Guayaquil; and we consulted them through a survey to know what was the impact that they considered of having over the central concept "chances of winning" to develop the necessary fuzzy rules later.

During this stage, each expert defines based on its criterion, the relationship existing between each pair of concepts, and for each causal relationship, it is obtained K number of rules under structure (see Fig. 5):

if C_i is A and C_j is B **then** W_{ij} is C,
end **if**

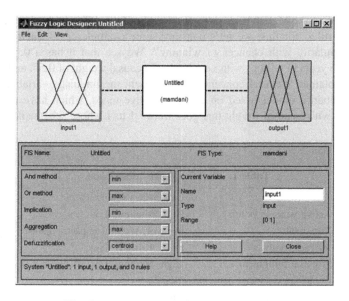

Fig. 5. Fuzzy Logic Designer with Mamdani.

Next, we use Matlab to create a fuzzy inference system, and through the centroid method and the Mamdani inference mechanism, we add the rules, and the obtained value from the de-diffusion is the value of the relationship. In Fig. 6, we present the interface of rules editor in Matlab Fuzzy Logic Designer.

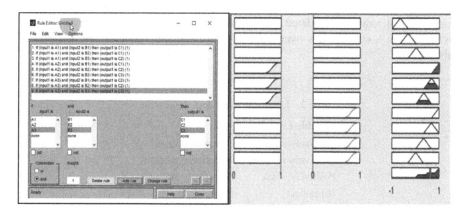

Fig. 6. Matlab editor rule.

After creating the Matlab rules, we get a weight of the different combinations given in our fuzzy rules, for this, we let's consider some example cases, such as the relationship "popularity with chances of winning". We see that it has a 0.63 of causal weight; active years in politics with vote bank of a causal weight of 0.55, and according to that, we obtained 9 causal concepts that represent the linguistic variables that will help us to obtain a model based on fuzzy cognitive maps, which have positive and negative axis with a causal weight that goes from −1 to 1 whose scheme is represented in Table 1.

Table 1. Causal concepts' description.

Symbol		Linguistic variable
C1	Active years in politics	High, Medium, Low
C2	Vote bank	In favor, Without impact, Against
C3	Internal conflicts	Fully, Partially, Not
C4	Proposal fulfillment	High, Medium, Low
C5	Campaign on social networks	Yes, No
C6	Currently in government	Yes, No
C7	Popularity	High, Medium, Low
C8	Development in performance	Good, Regular, Bad
C9	Chances of winning	Very high, High, Medium, Low, Very low

Causal relationships between such concepts have a weight that represents the influence degree of a concept A over a concept B, this is a fuzzy value in the scale between −1 and 1, being 0 the absence of a relationship between the concepts. Then, this numerical value is translated into a linguistic variable that describes the impact degree of that a concept has over another. The linguistic variables are described in Table 2.

Table 2. Linguistic variables' description.

Variable Lingüística	
Positively strong	Negatively weak
Positively medium	Negatively medium
Positively weak	Negatively strong
No impact	

3 Fuzzy Cognitive Maps (FCM)

The fuzzy cognitive maps (FCM) are graphs directed with fuzzy signs with feedbacks and can model the events, values, and objectives as a collection of concepts when forging a causal relationship between these concepts [25]. The models of fuzzy

cognitive maps are created as collections of concepts, and the various causal relationships that exist between these concepts. The concepts are represented by nodes and
causal relationships by arcs directed between the nodes. Each arc is accompanied by a
weight that defines the degree of causal relationship between the two nodes. The weight
sign determines the positive or negative causal relationship between the two concepts
or nodes.

3.1   Fuzzy Cognitive Map in Decision-Making

The fuzzy cognitive maps allow to analyze thematic contents about any discipline,
situations and also processes that intervene in the development of operative strategies,
providing a mental image taken from the environment, and which it can be resorted to
analyzing the changes that occur in the situation as being investigated when the original
environmental stimuli are modified [33].

Similarly, we can create models of causality supported under the criterion of
experts by using fuzzy cognitive maps, being these models useful for the analysis of
hypothetical scenarios based on the underlying structures of the concepts that have
more significant weight Causality related in this case to the facts that affect the
effectiveness of the strategies of electoral marketing.

3.2   Parameters' Definition

The nodes in fuzzy cognitive maps are represented by concepts that have causality and
might or not relate to an effect, these relationships between nodes are called causal
weight, and have a value between -1 to 1 where $W_{ij} > 0$ expresses positive causation,
while for W_{ij} ¡ 0 expresses negative causation, and $W_{ij} = 0$ does not express any
relationship (see Fig. 7) [5].

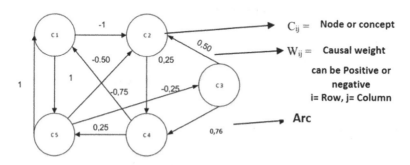

Fig. 7. Fuzzy Cognitive Map.

The steps to follow up to make the adjacency matrix extracted from the fuzzy
cognitive map, where C = concept, W = weight, i = row, j = column, are described in
Table 3.

Table 3. MCD adjacency matrix.

Ci/Cj	C1	C2	C3	C4	C5
C1	0	−1	0	0	1
C2	0	0	0	0,25	0
C3	0	0,5	0	0,75	0
C4	−0,75	0	0	0	0,25
C5	1	−0,5	−0,25	0	0

3.3   Fuzzy Cognitive Map Inference

In [32] indicated that each concept in the graph of the fuzzy cognitive map has an Ai value expressing the amount of its corresponding physical value. Hence, its causal weight, for example, the popularity concept weights 1 and derives from the transformation of the fuzzy values assigned by the experts to the numerical values. In other words, an expert group says that popularity has a very high causality on chances of winning. Thus, its final weight would be 1. Now, these values will be displayed in an array along with their concepts, called adjacency matrix, where Ci is the rows and Cj the columns. The Ai value of each Ci concept is calculated during each simulation step, calculating the influence of other concepts on the specific concept, selecting one of the following equations (inference rules):

Kosko inference rule:

$$A_i(k+1) = f\left(\sum_{j=1, J \neq 1}^{N} W_{ji} \; X \; A_j(k)\right) \tag{1}$$

Kosko inference rule modified:

$$A_i(k+1) = f\left(A_i(k) + \sum_{j=1, J \neq 1}^{N} W_{ji} \; x \; A_j(k)\right) \tag{2}$$

Rescaling inference rule:

$$A_i(k+1) = f\left((2 \; x \; A_i(k) - 1) + \sum_{j=1, J \neq 1}^{N} W_{ji} \; x \; (2 \; x \; A_j(k) - 1)\right) \tag{3}$$

3.4   Cognitive Map in Mental Modeler

Mental Modeler [17] has a web-based modeling application for support of group decision making, and might be used by non-experts and need to design a simple model and simulate its behavior for some scenarios the main disadvantage in the lack of learning algorithm and its limited set of experimental operations.

The fuzzy cognitive map details 9 causal concepts (Fig. 8), which have positive and negative arcs with a causal weight that goes from −1 to 1. Then, we determine the adjacency matrix with their respective weights (Table 4). Hence, we observe that the connections weights of arcs are directed towards each causal concept, and have an interval of −1 to 1, where Ci is the rows and Cj the columns. Ci increases causally to Cj if the weight is greater than 0, it decreases if the weight is less than 0, and has no effect if it is equal to 0. The causal concept C1 increases causally to the concepts C2, C4, C7, C8, and C9. The causal concept C2 increases causally to the C9 concept. The causal concept C3 decreases causally to the concepts C2, C7, and C9. The causal C4 concept increases causally to the concepts C2, C7, and C9. The causal C5 concept increases causally to the concepts of C7 and C9. The causal concept C6 increases causally to the concepts C4, C7, C8, and C9. The causal concept C7 increases causally to the concepts of C2 and C9. The causal concept C8 increases causally to the concepts C2, C7, and C9. The concepts of C1, C2, C4, C5, C6, C7 and C8 increase C9. The concept of C3 decreases C9.

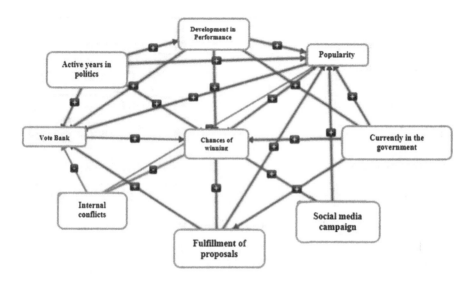

Fig. 8. MCD - Chances to win for political marketing.

Table 4. The adjacency matrix corresponding to MCD.

Concept	C1	C2	C3	C4	C5	C6	C7	C8	C9
C1	0	0,55	0	0,54	0	0	0,58	0,54	0,54
C2	0	0	0	0	0	0	0	0	0,46
C3	0	−0,21	0	0	0	0	−0,21	0	−0,76
C4	0	0,62	0	0	0	0	0,58	0	0,75
C5	0	0	0	0	0	0	0,58	0	0,77
C6	0	0	0	0,55	0	0	0,58	0,55	0,56
C7	0	0,58	0	0	0	0	0	0	0,81
C8	0	0,62	0	0	0	0	0,58	0	0,77
C9	0	0	0	0	0	0	0	0	0

4   Scenario Analysis in Mental Modeler

Scenario 1. Acandidate who has been in politics for a few years and had a vote bank against, and has few internal conflicts and who fulfills many proposals and who performs a good advertising campaign to pay social networks and is currently in government, and he is very popular and has a development in the middle performance. All these variables were entered into Mental Modeler obtaining; as a result, 98% of chances of winning (see Fig. 9).

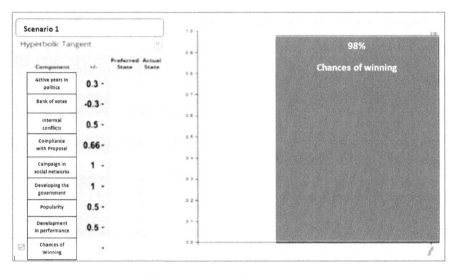

Fig. 9. Scenario 1. Chances to win.

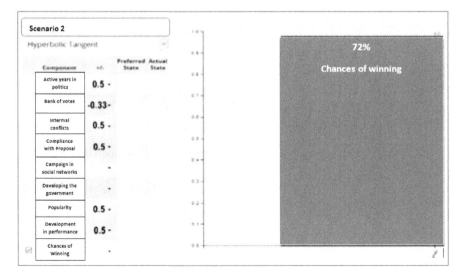

Fig. 10. Scenario 2. Chances to win.

Scenario 2. Acandidate who has not been in politics for many years and who has a vote bank against, and who has an average degree in internal conflicts and who fulfills some proposals, and who does not carry out a campaign on social networks, and who is not currently in the government, and he is something popular and has a development in the average performance. All these variables were entered into the Web application Mental Modeler obtaining; as a result, 72% of chances of winning (see Fig. 11).

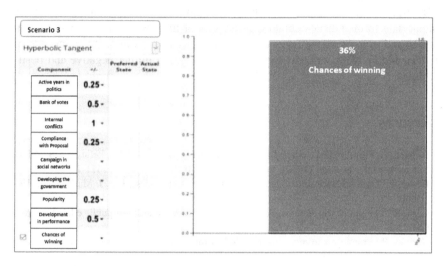

Fig. 11. Scenario 3. Chances to win.

Scenario 3. Acandidate who does not have years in politics and who has no bank of votes in favor, and who has many internal conflicts and who does not comply with the proposals, and who does not carry out a campaign on social networks of payment, and that is not currently in the Government and that does not is very popular and has a development in the middle performance. All these variables were entered into the Web application Mental Modeler obtaining; as a result, 36% of chances of winning (see Fig. 10).

5 Results

We obtained a fuzzy inference system that allowed acquiring the causal weights of the relations posed through diffuse rules created from the criterion of the experts. It was demonstrated by using fuzzy cognitive maps that corresponding concepts to the causal variables, these influence the decision making of the political marketing strategy. And it will be a great help to invest the capital intelligently based on data obtained, as an approach can be considered the carrying out of segmented campaigns, according to the geographic area and knowing the needs of the students. The student representatives can feed the model. The fuzzy cognitive map can be modified according to each expert criteria.

6 Conclusions

In this study, it was possible to model a fuzzy inference system allows creating events between different variables that correspond to the political marketing, helping to analyze the impact that a candidate might have for winning an election. For instance, the student representative, who has to know how to offer his/her solutions through an effective and quality campaign by listening to the needs of students in a specific market.

By using current technologies such as Facebook, and Twitter. Which might be used as input data from statistics obtained at the end of the advertising campaign for data analysis, and to improve the fuzzy cognitive map, in such a way that you can add new variables and collect comments from students analyzing further negative and positive causalities.

References

1. Bowler, S., Farrell, D.M. (eds.): Electoral Strategies and Political Marketing. CPS. Palgrave Macmillan UK, London (1992). https://doi.org/10.1007/978-1-349-22411-1
2. Butler, P., Collins, N.: Political marketing: structure and process. Eur. J. Mark. **28**(1), 19–34 (1994)
3. Carli, S.: The university student. Towards a history of the present of public education, p. 288 (2012)
4. Carlino, P.: Practices and representations of writing in the university: the cases of Australia, Canada, USA and Argentina (2009)
5. Carreiras, M.: Cognitive maps: Critical review. Psychol. Stud. **7**(26), 59–91 (1986)
6. Casillas, M., Chain, R., Jacome, N.: Social origin of students and student trajectories at the University of Veracruz. High School Magazine **36**(142), 7–29 (2007)
7. Castro Martínez, L.: Political marketing in the United States: the Obama case. North America **7**(1), 209–222 (2012)
8. Collins, N., Butler, P.: Considerations on market analysis for political parties. N. J. O'Shaughnessy, & SC Henneberg, The idea of political marketing, pp. 1–17 (2002)
9. Costales, J.R.: Rafael correa and the Elections 2006. Beginnings of marketing and digital political communication in ecuador. Chasqui Latin Am. J. Commun. (126), 116–123 (2014)
10. Dámazo, A.Y.P.: Negative campaigns in the 2000 and 2006 elections in Mexico. Mex. J. Polit. Soc. Sci. **59**(222), 87–115 (2014)
11. Darias, M., Gonzalez, M.: Prediction of personality voting behavior and sociopolitical factors. Polit. Psychol. Mag. **17**, 45–78 (1998)
12. Enríquez, I.G., Ramirez-Cortes, J., Ibarra, M., Gomez-Gil, P.: Autonomous tracking of the position of an object by neuro-diffuse vision and control in matlab. In: 6th International Congress of Investigation in Electrical and Electronic Engineering, pp. 3–7
13. Fernández Collado, C., Hernández Sampieri, R.: Election marketing and acting government image: how to achieve successful political campaigns (1999)
14. Fernández Poncela, A.M.: Elecciones, Jóvenes y política. Convergencia. Revista de Ciencias Sociales **6**(20) (1999)
15. Flores Ambrocio, M.C., Valentínez, L., Jessica, A., Reyes Montes, M.C.: Influencia del marketing político en los electores que votaron por primera vez en las elecciones federales del 2012, en la cabecera municipal de ixtlahuaca (2014)

16. Gönül, F.F., Hofstede, F.T.: How to compute optimal catalog mailing decisions. Mark. Sci. **25**(1), 65–74 (2006)
17. Gray, S.A., Gray, S., Cox, L.J., Henly-Shepard, S.: Mental modeler: a fuzzy-logic cognitive mapping modeling tool for adaptive environmental management. In: 2013 46th Hawaii International Conference on System Sciences (HICSS), pp. 965–973. IEEE (2013)
18. Gutiérrez, J.A.T., Acebrón, L.B., Casielles, R.V.: Investigación de mercados: métodos de recogida y análisis de la información para la toma de decisiones en marketing. Editorial Paraninfo (2005)
19. Guzman, D., Castaño, V.: La lógica difusa en ingeniería: principios, aplicaciones y futuro. Revista de Ciencia y Tecnología Vol. 24 Núm. 2 2009 (2009)
20. Hurtado, S.M., Gomez, G.P.: Modelo de inferencia difuso para estudio de crédito. Dyna **75** (154), 215–229 (2008)
21. Jermyn, M.G.: Method and apparatus for generating purchase incentive mailing based on prior purchase history, 15 Feb 2000, US Patent 6,026,370
22. Kenneth, C., Baack, D.: Publicidad, promoción y comunicación integral en marketing. Editorial Pearson, 3ª Edición, México (2010)
23. Lasswell, H.: La concepción emergente de las ciencias políticas. In: El estudio de las políticas Públicas, pp. 105–118. Porruà (2000)
24. Leyva-Vázquez, M., Santos-Baquerizo, E., Peña-González, M., Cevallos-Torres, L., Guijarro-Rodríguez, A.: The extended hierarchical linguistic model in fuzzy cognitive maps. In: Valencia-García, R., Lagos-Ortiz, K., Alcaraz-Mármol, G., del Cioppo, J., Vera-Lucio, N. (eds.) CITI 2016. CCIS, vol. 658, pp. 39–50. Springer, Cham (2016). https://doi.org/10.1007/978-3-319-48024-4_4
25. Leyva-Vazquez, M.Y., Rosado-Rosello, R., Febles-Estrada, A.: Modeling and analysis of the critical success factors of software projects through diffuse cognitive maps. Inf. Sci. pp. 41–46 (2012)
26. Lorenzo, I.F., Aguerrebere, P.M.: Gestión empresarial de la agencia de publicidad. IF Lorenzo, & PM Aguerrebere, Gesti´on empresarial de la agencia de publicidad (2014)
27. Maarek, P.J., Costa, P.O., et al.: Marketing político y comunicación: claves para una buena informacion política. Paidós, (1997)
28. Mair, P., Müller, W.C., Plasser, F.: One introduction: electoral challenges and party responses. Political parties and electoral change: Party responses to electoral markets, p. 1 (2004)
29. de Mantilla, L.F.: Qué evalúa el ciudadano al momento de votar?. algunas apre- ciaciones desde el enfoque racional. Reflexión política **10**(19) (2008)
30. Meza Martinez, M.M., Mulato Zuñiga, O.A., et al.: An´alisis a las estrategias de marketing político de Juan Manuel Santos durante la campaña presidencial del año 2014 en Colombia. B.S. thesis, Universidad Militar Nueva Granada (2017)
31. Montecinos, E.: Analisis del comportamiento electoral: De la elecci´on racional a la teor´ıa de redes. Revista de Ciencias Sociales **13**(1), 9–22 (2007)
32. Pérez García, R.: Algoritmo para optimizar la topología en un Mapa Cognitivo Difuso. Ph.D. thesis, Universidad Central Marta Abreu de Las Villas (2014)
33. Pérez-Teruel, K., Leyva-Vázquez, M., Espinilla, M., Estrada-Sentí, V.: Computación con palabras en la toma de decisiones mediante mapas cognitivos difusos. Revista Cubana de Ciencias Informáticas **8**(2), 19–34 (2014)
34. Recalde, P.: Elecciones presidenciales 2006: una aproximaci´on a los actores del proceso. Iconos. Revista de Ciencias Sociales (27) (2007)
35. Roche, L.M.: Modelos de comportamiento electoral: "por qué las personas votan de una manera y no de otra" GestioPolis (2008). http://www.gestiopolis.com/economia/modelos-de-comportamiento-electoral.html. 22 de febrero-2015

36. Ross, T.J.: Fuzzy Logic with Engineering Applications. Wiley, Chichester (2009)
37. Samaniego Alcívar, C.A.: Análisis de la aplicación de una estrategia de comunicacion por parte del gobierno central periodo 2008–2013. B.S. thesis, Quito: Universidad Israel, 2015 (2015)
38. Soto Camargo, A.M., Medina Hurtado, S.: Desarrollo de un sistema de inferencia difuso para la evaluación de crédito por parte de una empresa prestadora de servicios. Dyna **71**(143) (2004)
39. Subirats, J.: Los dilemas de una relación inevitable. innovación democrática y tecnologías de la información y de la comunicación. H. CAIRO CAROU (comp.). Democracia digital. Límites y oportunidades. Barcelona: Trotta. Pág pp. 89–114 (2002)
40. Túñez, M., Sixto, J.: Redes sociales, política y compromiso 2.0: La comunicación de los diputados españoles en facebook. Revista Latina de comunicación social (66) (2011)
41. Vazquez, J.G., Castilloa, O., Aguilar, L.: Sintesis de funciones de membresia trape- zoidales para implementacion de controladores de lggica difusa. In: HAFSA Internacional Conference on Fuzzy Systems, Neural Networks and Genetic Algorithms (2005)
42. Zadeh, L.A.: Fuzzy logic computing with words. IEEE Trans. Fuzzy Syst. **4**(2), 103–111 (1996)

Data Analysis Algorithms
for Revenue Assurance

Gilberto F. Castro[1,2]([✉]) [iD], Fausto R. Orozco[1] [iD], Giselle L. Núñez[1],
Anié Bermudez-Peña[3] [iD], Alfonso A. Guijarro[1], and Mirella C. Ortíz[1]

[1] Facultad de Ciencias Matemáticas y Físicas, Universidad de Guayaquil,
Guayaquil, Ecuador
{gilberto.castroa,fausto.orozcol,giselle.nunezn,
alfonso.guijarror,mirella.ortizz}@ug.edu.ec
[2] Facultad de Ingeniería, Universidad Católica Santiago de Guayaquil,
Guayaquil, Ecuador
gilberto.castro@cu.ucsg.edu.ec
[3] Facultad 2, Universidad de las Ciencias Informáticas, Havana, Cuba
abp@uci.cu

Abstract. In companies there are dissimilar factors that influence the loss of income, such as errors in planning, in decision-making, inadequate control of projects and poor treatment of inaccuracy and uncertainty in the data. Some of these causes can be mitigated if anomalous data contained in the information systems of the organizations themselves are analyzed. Present research proposes several algorithms to support revenue assurance in project management organizations. As a novelty, this proposal combines outlier mining, proactive risk management and soft computing techniques. A variety of algorithms for detection of anomalous data in revenue assurance is implemented in a library based on free software. These algorithms apply methods based on data spatial analysis, K-means, Mahalanobis and Euclidean distances, partial clustering with automatic estimation of the clusters number, pattern recognition techniques, heuristics, among others. In the research, cross-validation tests, non-parametric tests and evaluation by a group of experts are carried out. For the application of the proposal in a real environment, databases of finished projects are used and the identification of situations generating anomalous data in project-oriented organizations is achieved. In addition, the proposal has been implemented in a computer tool dedicated to project management with which several companies and centers of development of information technologies have benefited, with more than 300 projects and 5000 users.

Keywords: Revenue assurance · Data analysis · Project management

1 Introduction

Currently, one of the forms of organization that has gained strength is integrated management of projects, due to its applicability in different scenarios. This has led to the proliferation of project management organizations in different areas of society and standards such as the Project Management Body of Knowledge (PMBOK) [1] and

© Springer Nature Switzerland AG 2019
M. Botto-Tobar et al. (Eds.): ICCCE 2018, CCIS 959, pp. 139–154, 2019.
https://doi.org/10.1007/978-3-030-12018-4_11

Capability Maturity Model Integration (CMMI) [2] that reflect good practices for project management.

Project management organizations are those that develop new products or services, organizing human and material resources in form of projects with well-defined objectives, start and end dates. A study carried out by Standish Group International, showed that historically, the numbers of projects satisfactorily managed, renegotiated and canceled, have moved by around 29%, 52% and 19% respectively [3]. An important element that must be analyzed beyond the number of renegotiated or failed projects is the economic and social impact of the same ones.

Despite efforts to improve management efficiency of these organizations, there are still many difficulties that generate income losses. Among the fundamental causes of project failure, shortcomings are identified in the planning, control, and monitoring processes, as well as scarce mechanisms for risk management and human resources management. Some of these causes can be mitigated if the anomalous data contained in information systems of the organizations themselves are analyzed.

Associated with the discipline of revenue assurance [4–8], aimed at the protection and recovery of financial resources in companies, the following deficiencies have been identified:

- Dependency of human resources to carry out revenue assurance, which introduces uncertainty in decisions and possible errors of operation.
- In project management organizations, phenomena such as heterogeneity in data, imprecision and uncertainty are presented.
- These situations are not adequately managed with traditional revenue assurance techniques; which affects effectiveness in the detection of anomalous situations that generate income losses.
- Inaccuracy in this scenario is shown in the in-completeness and noise in data. Uncertainty arises because data recorded depends to a large extent on perception and expertise of systems users.
- Frequently proposed solutions are based only on reactive approaches and do not adequately use active or proactive strategies of revenue assurance; affecting in this way the efficiency of detection processes of anomalous situations.
- Difficulties in dealing with high dynamism, continuous improvement and diversity of project management organizations.
- Often the implemented solutions constitute black boxes supported by proprietary tools that affect the technological sovereignty of organizations. Full impact of information management with these external tools is not known for sure.

It has been identified that many of these problems affect efficiency and effectiveness of revenue assurance from the perspective of ability to detect anomalous data. Next, concepts of efficiency and effectiveness used in this research are introduced:

Efficiency evaluates the time used by algorithms for the detection of anomalous data in processes of revenue assurance.

Effectiveness reflects the ability to detect anomalous situations in data, usually caused by fraud actions or operational failures, or detection and estimation of risks that affect income.

Present research proposes several algorithms to support revenue assurance in project management organizations. It allows for the identification of situations that generate anomalous data in said organizations. Risk management techniques, anomalous data mining and soft computing are thus combined. The application of the proposal includes a library of algorithms for the detection of anomalous data in revenue assurance, which has been implemented in a computer tool dedicated to project management.

This paper is organized in the following parts. Section 2 presents the main elements of revenue assurance in project management organizations and the bases of algorithms applied in data analysis. Section 3 exemplifies how revenue assurance is affected by the algorithms used for predicting and detecting anomalous situations. Section 4 discusses a real scenario's results of the application and validation of this proposal. Finally, conclusions and future works are presented.

2 Related Works

2.1 Project Management and Revenue Assurance

The greatest advancement in the development of project management discipline has been the creation of schools or institutions dedicated to the formalization and standardization to develop new methods of organization and work. Among these institutions is Project Management Institute (PMI) with its PMBOK standard [1], Software Engineering Institute (SEI) with the CMMI standard [2], International Project Management Association (IPMA) [9] and International Organization for Standardization (ISO) with its standards 10006 and 21500 [10].

These institutions along with their respective standards of project management relate both the generic and specific practices applicable to management; however, they do not propose concrete algorithms to achieve it. Mostly, they are based on manual work and the exhaustive documentation of processes, rather than the determination of faults and errors by data analysis. In general, they do not allow an adequate treatment of uncertainty and ambiguity existing in management. The sixth version of PMBOK [1] proposes new techniques for risk management in projects. Through quantitative risk analysis, treatment of uncertainty and data analysis is achieved.

On the other hand, revenue assurance combines a set of techniques, policies, and models, with the objective of increasing revenues and reducing costs for organizations that apply it, following reactive and proactive approaches. It is shown as an interdisciplinary area where all the following converge: databases technologies, statistics, anomalous data mining, soft computing, and emerging computing techniques.

Regarding computational techniques used for revenue assurance, both TMForum and GRAPA acknowledge the use of anomalous data mining techniques [4–8]. The following Table 1 gives a summary of most used computational techniques. Yet in most cases, big companies hire consulting firms, which generally implement revenue assurance procedures according to their own methods. Among the most used techniques are: application of expert judgment and application of production rules proposed by experts, generally very specific for each scenario.

Table 1. Techniques most used in revenue assurance processes

Processes	Anomalous data mining techniques used
Risk analysis	Sampling, Group analysis, Distribution analysis, Central tendency analysis, Regression
Early detection	Sampling, Group analysis, Chaid/Cart, RNA
Design of controls	Sampling, Chaid/Cart, Distribution analysis, Central tendency analysis
Root cause analysis	Group analysis, Distribution analysis, Central tendency analysis
Forecast	Sampling, Group Analysis, Chaid/Cart, RNA, Regression

2.2   Analysis of Anomalous Data

In this section, some of data analysis and anomalous data mining techniques are discussed. Anomalous data, or outlier, is defined as an observation that deviates greatly from other observations, appearing as a suspicious subject that could be generated by mechanisms different from the rest of data [11].

The techniques for the detection of anomalous data are shown in different application scenarios [12–18] among which are: detection of fraud in credit cards and telecommunications, errors in planning, detection of prices of products handled, processing of images, fraud in clinical trials, analysis of irregularities in voting processes, detection of network intruders, criminal analysis in other areas.

For data analysis and outlier identification, several methods with different approaches and classifications were studied. Suggested below are methods based on distance, clustering, spatial data analysis, and active learning.

Distance-based methods: they allow to detect the proximity between points. They consider as anomalous data, those points with greater distance to the rest of their neighbors. Euclidean distance and Mahalanobis distance are used, reporting better results. They have been widely used for the detection of anomalous data in spaces of high dimensionality [19]. Heuristics and indexes have also been proposed that help to reduce the complexity of algorithms and the number of comparisons required in traditional distance-based methods [20]. They achieve the following advantages: they do not need to know a priori the distribution of data and they can be applied in search spaces on which a measure of distance can be defined. These methods generally allow a greater level of granularity than other methods, facilitating the differentiation between noisy data and anomalous data.

Clustering-based methods, especially those based on partitions: perform successive divisions of data set. Objects are organized into k groups, so that the deviation of each object must be minimized in relation to the center of group [21]. K-means is one of the most used algorithms for the formation of clusters. Classical K-means depends on a priori selection of the number of groups and the centroids. Main advantage of clustering-based methods is that they allow a global data analysis, detecting small groups of isolated data [22]. Main limitation is that sometimes they cannot discern clearly if they are in presence of really anomalous data or if they are noisy data.

Methods based on spatial analysis of data: they are quite close to clustering methods. They are based on the principle that an anomalous data in space is an object that, by representing its attributes in space, these are significantly different from their neighboring objects. In this category are graphic methods; these are based on spatial visualization of data, their implementation is easier in spaces of low dimensionality [11]. Especially methods based on angles, assume that anomalous data are those that when forming different angles with any of the rest of points of the data set, it is found that amplitude of said angles does not vary significantly. This method is based on relationship between the distance of points and cosine of the inscribed angle between segments that form said points [23].

Method based on active learning: data are classified by iterations [24]. In each iteration only a few data sets are identified and classified with the intervention of human experts who classify or ratify the classification made by algorithms of data analyzed. In first iteration unsupervised methods are used, already classified data can be used using supervised techniques in new iterations. Some difficulties associated with these methods are uncertainty and ambiguity during first iterations. Expert consensus techniques can be used in these cases to reduce the possibility of uncertainty in classifications and guarantee an adequate learning of the behavior patterns of anomalous data identified.

Distance-based methods report their best results in scenarios with relatively small data, unlike other proximity-based methods. The starkest difference between these methods and those based on clustering is in granularity used during analysis process, an element that sometimes allows distance-based algorithms to be more robust [25].

It can be concluded that there are no deterministic or unique solutions for revenue assurance applicable to all organizations. This occurs as each scenario presents variables, internal and external factors, with a high impact on revenues and decisions for their management.

3   Data Analysis Algorithms for Revenue Assurance

This section coherently presents a method by which applies data analysis algorithms to the revenue assurance of project management organizations (see Fig. 1). The method is based on an analysis and processing of data that reflects the activity of a particular organization analyzed. It consists of five stages that are described below.

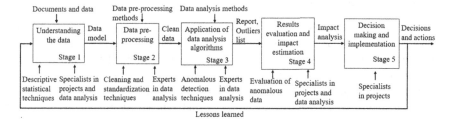

Fig. 1. Data analysis method for revenue assurance

Stage 1: consists of two parts. At first, the source of data and organization processes must be understood in order to define a taxonomy that helps to identify the situations that affect revenue assurance as possible causes of failures, frauds or leaks. In a second action, a data model collected from the information systems of organization is constructed; and the nature of data, existence of missing values and most frequent errors in them is analyzed.

Stage 2: employs descriptive statistics techniques combined with the facilities of the information systems and the SQL language for data recovery. In this stage, different activities related to data pre-processing, such as cleaning, standardization and selection of attributes (both descriptors and decision makers) that will make up the information system, are grouped together.

Stage 3: application and modeling of data analysis algorithms for detection of situations that reflect loss of income. It relies on active and reactive approaches. These approaches are guaranteed by the agility of response of the proposed algorithms which is also one of the variables analyzed in this research. Anomalous data are detected based on a strategy of independent treatment of data with multiple algorithms and then the union of results. Several iterations are carried out and in each one an algorithm specialized in the detection of a type of anomalous situation is applied. Once all the algorithms have been executed, the results found are combined.

Stage 4: for evaluate the results and estimation of impact, it is proposed to use some of the following techniques: estimation by analogy, estimation by three values, parametric estimation, expert judgment or analysis of the costs of revenue assurance. Cost estimation by analogy uses historical information based on the experience of previous projects and the impact of certain factors on them. Estimation by three values is based on: the most probable cost given by a realistic evaluation of expert; optimistic cost based on the best possible scenario with least possible impact; and the pessimistic cost based on the analysis of worst case scenario. Parametric estimation uses a statistical relationship between historical data and other variables to calculate an estimate of economic impact.

Stage 5: information systems is proposed for generate reports and a system of recommendations to help users in making decisions. Each anomalous data identified will be framed in some of situations that affect the income, the recommendation system is based on content and returns the measures that can be taken in each situation. During decision making, results are collected in form of lessons learned; this allows the continuous improvement and sustainability in the application of revenue assurance techniques in the organization.

The proposed method requires, for its implementation, presence of people with knowledge of data analysis and revenue assurance, since it combines project management techniques with anomalous data mining techniques to detect situations that affect revenue assurance processes in organizations.

Different techniques and algorithms are applied to project management databases, discovering causal relationships and effective and efficient combinations to detect anomalous situations that generate income losses. Below is the Meta algorithm designed to combine the results of multiple algorithms.

3.1   Meta Algorithm Based on the Combination of Different Techniques

```
1. AlgorithmBasedCombinationMethods (D, A)
   Inputs: D: represents the data set to be analyzed
           A: represents the set of algorithms, where A_i is an
           algorithm and denotes A_i ∈ A
           A_active: represents an active learning algorithm with
           intervention of experts
2. Start
   3. i =1
   4. D_i = D
   5. Until remain algorithms without doing, in opposite case go
   to step 11
      6. Select the A_i algorithm
      7. Select the data set from the original set Di = D
      8. P_i = A_i(D_i) // Detection of possible anomalous data
      9. i ++
   10. Go back to step 5
   11. O_i = A_active(P_i)•i // Application of active learning to veri-
   fy anomalous data
   12. O = ∪ O_i // combination of anomalous data detected in each
   iteration
   13. Return anomalous data contained in O and mark them for
   learning
  14. End
```

A summary of the algorithms used in data analysis is presented below. They are all applied in order to find those that report best results for each specific problem.

Angle. It is based on spatial analysis approach of data, in particular a method based on angles. Performs the detection of anomalous values based on angles in a specified data frame. This algorithm is recommended for high dimensionality scenarios [23].

Cross-clustering. It is based on partial clustering with automatic estimation of clusters number and identification of outliers, combined with evolutionary algorithms, provides automatic estimation of groups and automatic estimation of anomalous elements. It calculates a partial clustering algorithm that combines the minimum variance algorithms and the Ward complete coupling, providing an automatic estimation of an adequate number of clusters and identification of atypical elements [26].

Kmodr. It is based on the use of simultaneous clustering methods. It is an implementation of K-means algorithm with a unified approach to group and detect outliers [22]. It is useful to create potentially tighter groups than standard K-means and simultaneously find anomalous data at low cost in a multidimensional space.

Distance_mahalanobis. It is based on Mahalanobis distance. It has as inputs nearest number of neighbors and data set. It uses a maximum distance function, concept of neighborhood and allows work with dynamic thresholds refining the search, by default it is the identity function. Returns anomalous data ordered downwards according to the distance to its nearest neighbors.

Kmeans_euclidean. It is a hybrid algorithm, based on K-means clustering combined with Euclidean distance. It has as inputs the number of expected centers and the data set. It uses Euclidean distance function and a cut threshold. It calculates the centers of founded clusters and returns anomalous data found.

Kmeans_norm_euclidean. It is a hybrid algorithm, similar to the Kmeans_euclidean algorithm, but works with normalized input data.

Kmeans_stats. This is a hybrid algorithm that combines clustering techniques with distance-based methods and pattern recognition techniques. It has as input the data set and a set of centers planted. Returns the list of anomalous data for which distance is greater than threshold. To improve the efficiency of this algorithm, it is used as a strategy to plant the centers initially according to the types of tasks, taking into account the information of problem in question. The calculation of threshold is also used to reduce the number of comparisons in algorithm.

Combine_outlier. It is a hybrid algorithm that combines clustering techniques based on heuristics and descriptive statistics techniques. The algorithm calculates a list of attributes ordered by degree of dispersion for each group. It applies active learning to determine clusters with anomalous data. To improve the efficiency of this algorithm, knowledge of the application scenario is used to know in advance the number of groups expected, knowledge that is used for the search by subspaces.

Active Learning. It runs at the end of applying the rest of algorithms to detect anomalous data. This receives as input the list of data suspected of being anomalous. At this moment, the experts in revenue assurance of the organization, validate if the suspect data are really anomalous or not and the analyzed data are marked. In addition, lessons are learned to be used in future analysis processes. Fundamental technique to be applied in this case is expert judgment.

To carry out a proactive strategy in revenue assurance, risks management in organization is proposed. Experts evaluate each of identified risks and computer with words techniques are used to measure the impact that these risks have on the income. Applied during the feasibility analysis of preliminary project, it can help eliminate risk situations in projects. Early detection of anomalous situations improves management of contracts and communication with customers. Satisfied clients for project compliance, for the detection and early correction of situations that affect project: they enable new business and contracts, they contribute to raising the income. The fulfillment of contracts, thanks to detect problems and good control, avoids claims and economic penalty saving income. For more details of the method proposed, consult [27].

4 Evaluation and Results

To validate this proposal, methodological triangulation techniques were used, combining the triangulation of data, methods, and experts. For this, several experiments were carried out and cross validation was applied in order to determine the best configuration of algorithms and compare them with respect to efficiency and effectiveness to detect anomalous situations in different databases. Finally, the application of the proposal in a case study was validated by experts.

Algorithms were compared from analyzing their performance with the databases: alone_rate, col_mix, mul_plan, mul_rate, mul_mix from the repository of Research Laboratory in Project Management [27], at the University of Computer Sciences. Databases are composed of 23 attributes and over 9000 records, 5% of which carry anomalous data. Each of these five databases was divided into 20 partitions to apply cross-validation techniques.

To compare the experiments, normality tests were performed using the Shapiro-Wilk test [28], and both parametric and non-parametric techniques were applied depending on normality analysis of the data. To carry out all tests, R language and its algorithm libraries were used. The Shapiro-Wilk test proved that samples do not meet a normal distribution with a p-value = 0.00032. The populations formed by the results of algorithms were compared using the nonparametric Wilcoxon test for two samples related to a 95% confidence interval [29].

Using the 20 partitions of the five databases and 53 configurations of the algorithms, 5300 experiments were performed, shown in Table 2.

Table 2. Parameters configurations for each algorithm

Algorithms	Algorithms parameters
Angle	$k \in \{3, 5, 7, 9\}$ Threshold $\rho \in \{0.92, 0.95\}$
Cross-clustering	$k\_min \in \{3, 4, 5\}$ $k\_max \in \{5, 7, 9\}$
Mahalanobis	$k \in \{3, 5, 7, 9\}$ Threshold $\rho \in \{0.92, 0.95\}$
Kmeans_euclidean	$k \in \{3, 5, 7, 9\}$ Threshold $\rho \in \{0.92, 0.95\}$
Kmeans_norm_euclidean	$k \in \{3, 5, 7, 9\}$ $\rho \in \{0.92, 0.95\}$
Kmeans_stats	$k \in \{3, 5, 7, 9\}$
Kmodr	$k \in \{3, 5, 7, 9\}$
Combine_outlier	$k \in \{5, 7\}$ $\rho \in \{0.92, 0.95\}$

To validate effectiveness, algorithms were compared with respect to the percent variable of anomalous data correctly detected where accuracy and recall metrics were used. Accuracy is defined as the percent of reported anomalous data, see Eq. (1) while recall is the percent of reported anomalous data regarding the amount of true anomalous data, see Eq. (2).

$$Accuracy_{(\rho)} = 100 \frac{|S(\rho) \cap T|}{S(\rho)} \qquad (1)$$

$$Recall_{(\rho)} = 100 \frac{|S(\rho) \cap T|}{T} \qquad (2)$$

Where ρ is the recovery threshold of outliers on the ordered list of possible anomalous data, $S(\rho)$ denotes the set of outliers retrieved, while T represents the set of true outliers. Accuracy and Recall metrics are combined based on the application of an OWA operator [30]. Figure 2 shows that algorithms Kmeans_stats and Combine_outlier have very similar results in all databases, except for collective anomalous data (col_mix), where Combine_outlier algorithm is slightly higher. The worst result was Kmeans_euclidean_9_0.92. The numbers after the algorithm means the training parameters (presented in Table 2); in this case, 9 is the number of expected centers, and 0.92 is the percentile value to determine the distance threshold.

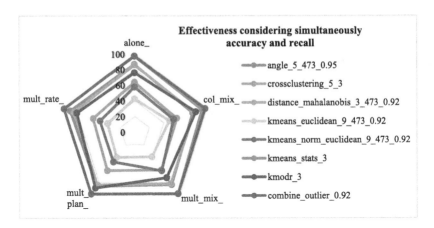

Fig. 2. Effectiveness of algorithms considering accuracy and recall simultaneously. Larger area corresponds to better results.

To compare the efficiency (time used by algorithms to detect anomalous data), Wilcoxon test found significant differences, with better results for Kmeans_stats and Distance_mahalanobis algorithms. While worst results are presented by Angle and Cross-clustering. Figure 3 shows the efficiency of the algorithms with respect to the databases used.

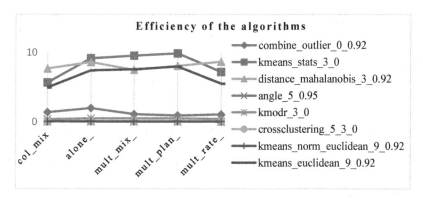

Fig. 3. Stability in algorithms efficiency

To evaluate the applicability of algorithms, experts were polled about several criteria that are shown in Table 3. Experts were selected from among several specialists in telecommunications company assurance and project management departments. Experts were asked to evaluate each measure using the following set of linguistic terms

Table 3. Result of expert evaluation about the application of the algorithms

Measures	Result of applying 2-tuples	Variance in experts response
M1. Level of integration with good project management practices	(High; 0.36)	0.24
M2. Proactive approach to revenue assurance	(High; 0.48)	0.26
M3. Reactive approach based on outlier mining	(Very High; −0.24)	0.19
M4. Active approach based on outlier mining	(Medium; −0.04)	0.21
M5. Treatment of imprecision and uncertainty in decision making	(High; −0.48)	0.26
M6. Application of data cleansing techniques prior to making decisions	(High; −0.24)	0.19
M7. Reuse level based on obtaining algorithm libraries	(High; 0.32)	0.23
M8. Level of use of open source technologies, promoting the reuse and technological sovereignty of organizations	(Very High; −0.28)	0.21
M9. Implementation in project management scenarios	(High; 0.12)	0.28
M10. Ease for generalization in different project management environments (construction, computing, research, training)	(Medium; −0.32)	0.39
M11. Effectiveness with respect to the detection of anomalous data	(High; 0.32)	0.23
M12. Efficiency with respect to response times	(High; 0.48)	0.26

LBTL = {None, Very Low, Low, Medium, High, Very High, and Perfect}. To standardize the expert evaluation with respect to each measure, 2-tuples model of computing with words was used. Table 3 shows the results of expert evaluation aggregation.

Experts positively evaluated the algorithms for revenue assurance and it is reflected in the High score of most criteria.

An experiment is carried out to validate the risk management proposal proactively associated with revenue losses. The traditional technique proposed in the PMBOK (Risk-PMBOK) is compared with the technique based on the 2-tuples model of computing with words (Risk-CWW) proposed. A group of six project management experts who did not participate in the selected projects were designated for validation. The experts consulted for risk assessment are characterized by: 4 PhD's and 2 Masters; regarding years of experience: 18.8 on average, 9.8 standard deviation, 14 minimum years and 37 maximum years dedicated.

Eighteen of the most common risks in this scenario were taken into account, covering all knowledge areas of project management. Finally, the mean squared errors calculated according to each method (Risk-PMBOK, Risk-CWW) were compared for each project. As shown in Fig. 4, the best results are obtained with the Risk-CWW assessment method.

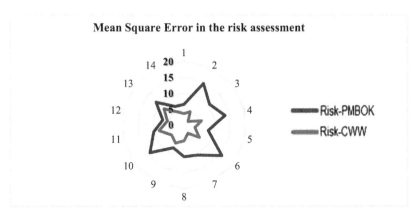

Fig. 4. Radial graph that represents the mean square error in the risk assessment (a smaller area indicates better algorithm)

Among advantages of the proposed method, there is the ease interpretation of the results when both evaluations of experts and final results are expressed in words. The proposed method also allows the simultaneous assessment of multiple experts. For more details, consult [27].

Some of the anomalous situations detected are shown below:

- Situation 1: the records of tasks that do not have assigned resources with the required competences or that due to their volume, require more human resources than those assigned.

- Situation 2: the records of tasks whose time or cost estimate is above or well below the predicted values.
- Situation 3: the records of tasks that do not respect in the chronogram the logical precedence or that have an excessively high waiting clearance with respect to other tasks.
- Situation 4: the requirements records in the work breakdown structure of the project for which there are no tasks recorded in the project schedule, dedicated to the development of the same.
- Situation 5: project records that, although similar to others because of their scope, may have estimated costs well above average.
- Situation 6: the recorded schedules that show an overload of human or non-human resources in multiple project development scenarios simultaneously.

The proposed method was implemented on the GESPRO platform due to its versatility and number of functionalities for revenue assurance [31, 32], among which are:

- Data analysis and revenue assurance module, which integrates libraries in R for the outlier detection.
- Risk management module, appropriate for proactive analysis.
- Scorecard with indicators and early warnings, aimed at detecting shortcomings in the planning and projects execution.
- Reach and quality management regarding the coverage of the requirements in the schedule and quality control.
- Project costs management and project costs prediction based on the data behavior.

Figure 5 shows a view of the risk management module as part of revenue assurance subsystem in the GESPRO tool.

| CATEGORÍAS DE RIESGO | ESTADOS DE RIESGOS | RIESGOS |

Riesgos del Centro

▸ Filtros

#	Nombre	Categoría	Estado	Prob.	Impacto	Detec.	Exposición	Evaluaciones
2	Pérdida de recursos humanos	Human resource management	Identify	(Bajo; 0.0)	(Alto; 0.0)	(Muy alto; 0.0)	(Medio; 0.0)	⊙ 1 ⚲ Ver
1	Planificacion sobre costos	Financial management	Identify	(Medio; 0)	(Medio; 0)	(Medio: 0)	(Medio; 0.0)	⊙ 0
3	Pérdida de Recursos Humanos	Human resource management	Identify	(Alto; 0.0)	(Alto; 0.0)	(Medio; 0.0)	(Medio; 0.0)	⊙ 2 ⚲ Ver
4	Dificultades con fenómenos ...	Natural Disasters	Analized	(Bajo; 0.0)	(Alto; 0.0)	(Bajo; 0.0)	(Medio; 0.0)	⊙ 1 ⚲ Ver

(1-4/4)

Fig. 5. View of risk management in GESPRO as part of revenue assurance subsystem

Another advantage in the use of free software as a requirement to achieve technological sovereignty, which helps ensure national development in a comprehensive and sustainable manner. Computational environment and functionalities developed on open source software technologies promote and reflect these precepts. This implies the following advantages for management tool: full domain of functionalities, detection of errors and corrections on time, continuous improvement based on collaborative development.

With the integration of the algorithms proposed in GESPRO platform, a total of five companies and fourteen information-technology development centers benefit, where approximately 300 projects are managed annually. An average of 5000 users of the tool are favored, with different levels of specialization and roles. Thanks to the use of the proposal, decision-making with help of GESPRO tool is currently carried out in a comfortable, integral and agile way, raising the quality of user's life.

5   Conclusions and Future Work

To determine the application of revenue assurance techniques, the specificities of each scenario and the nature of its data must be considered. A method was presented that allows the detection for anomalous situations that generates income losses in project-oriented organizations, based on the combination of project management techniques, anomalous data mining, and soft computing. Hybrid algorithms were designed to take advantage of distance-based strategies with tools based on clustering and heuristics. A library of data analysis algorithms based on free software was developed and integrated into GESPRO platform, an element that enables its application in real scenarios with high economic and social impact. It is shown that in the databases used for experimentation, the algorithm with best results regarding efficacy and efficiency was Kmeans_stats. Integral evaluation of the method showed that it complies with all the indicators expected to be analyzed. Further research should be done, however, on the application of the proposed method in real-time scenarios using strategies for high-performance computing.

References

1. PMI: A Guide to the Project Management Body of Knowledge. PMBOK® Guide, vol. 6th edn. Project Management Institute, Pennsylvania (2017)
2. CMMI Product Team: CMMI for Development, Version 1.3. Software Engineering Institute, Carnegie Mellon University, Pittsburgh, Pennsylvania, Technical Report CMU/SEI-2010-TR-033 (2010). http://resources.sei.cmu.edu/library/asset-view.cfm?AssetID=9661
3. The Standish Group International: Standish Group 2015 Chaos Report. The Standish Group International Inc., New York (2015)
4. TMForum: Revenue Assurance a survey pre-result blog: Lack of cross-functional mandate holds back change, say Revenue Assurance professionals (2015)
5. Acosta, K.: Aseguramiento de ingresos: una actividad fundamental en las empresas de telecomunicaciones. Revista Ingeniería Industrial **29**(2), 1–6 (2008)
6. Mattison, R.: The Telco Revenue Assurance Handbook. XiT Press, Oakwood Hills, Illinois, USA (2005). http://www.grapatel.com/A-GRAPA/07-Library/RABook.asp#top
7. Mattison, R.: The Revenue Assurance Standards, Release 2009, GRAPA. XiT Press, Oakwood Hills (2009)

8. GRAPA: The Global Revenue Assurance Professional Association (GRAPA) Professionalizing the Information, Communications and Technology Industry (2016)

9. IPMA: International Project Management Association (2017). http://www.ipma.world/

10. ISO: ISO 21500:2012 Guidance on Project Management. International Organization for Standardization (2012)

11. Ben-Gal, I.: Outlier detection. Data Mining and Knowledge Discovery Handbook: A Complete Guide for Practitioners and Researchers. Kluwer Academic Publishers. Department of Industrial Engineering, Tel-Aviv University (2005)

12. Deneshkumar, V., Senthamaraikannan, V., et al.: Identification of outliers in medical diagnostic system using data mining techniques. Int. J. Stat. Appl. **4**(6), 241–248 (2014). https://doi.org/10.5923/j.statistics.20140406.01

13. Chen, X.: Optimizing MPBSM Resource Allocation Based on Revenue Management: A China Mobile Information Systems. Hindawi Publishing Corporation, vol. 2015, Article ID 892705, 10 pp (2015). https://doi.org/10.1155/2015/892705

14. Guerriero, F., Miglionico, G., et al.: Strategic and operational decisions in restaurant revenue management. Eur. J. Oper. Res. **237**(3), 1119–1132 (2014). https://doi.org/10.1016/j.ejor.2014.02.048

15. Ferrara, E., De Meo, P., et al.: Detecting criminal organizations in mobile phone networks. Expert Syst. Appl. **41**(13), 5733–5757 (2014). https://doi.org/10.1016/j.eswa.2014.03.024

16. Manish, G., Jing, G., et al.: Outlier Detection for Temporal Data (2014). https://doi.org/10.2200/s00573ed1v01y201403dmk008

17. Souza, A.M., Amazonas, J.R.: An outlier detect algorithm using big data processing and internet of things architecture. Procedia Comput. Sci. **52**, 1010–1015 (2015). https://doi.org/10.1016/j.procs.2015.05.095

18. Barmade, A., Nashipudinath, M.M.: An efficient strategy to detect outlier transactions. Int. J. Soft Comput. Eng. **3**(6), 174–178 (2014). https://doi.org/10.1109/ICSMC.2011.6084075

19. Ghoting, A., Parthasarathy, S., Otey, M.E.: Fast mining of distance-based outliers in high-dimensional datasets. In: International Conference on Data Mining. Society for Industrial and Applied Mathematics (2006). https://doi.org/10.1137/1.9781611972764.70

20. Ramaswamy, S., Rastogi, R., Shim, K.: Efficient algorithms for mining outliers from large data sets. ACM Sigmod Rec. **29**(2), 427–438 (2000). https://doi.org/10.1145/335191.335437

21. Vijendra, S., Shivani, P.: Robust Outlier Detection Technique in Data Mining: A Univariate Approach. Faculty of Engineering and Technology, Mody Institute of Technology and Science, India (2014)

22. Chawla, S. Gionis, A.: K-means: a unified approach to clustering and outlier detection. In: SIAM International Conference on Data Mining (2013). https://doi.org/10.1137/1.9781611972832.21

23. Kriegel, H-P., Schubert, M., et al.: Angle-based outlier detection in high dimensional data. In: KDD 2008, Las Vegas, Nevada (2008). doi:978-1-60558-193-4/08/08

24. Pelleg, D., Moore, A.W.: Active learning for anomaly and rare-category detection. In: NIPS 2004 Proceedings of the 17th International Conference on Neural Information Processing Systems, Vancouver, Canada, pp. 1073–1080 (2004)

25. Zimmermann, A.: A feature construction framework based on outlier detection and discriminative pattern mining. CoRR, arXiv: 1407.4668, pp. 1–11 (2014)

26. Tellaroli, P., Bazzi, M., et al.: CrossClustering: a partial clustering algorithm with automatic estimation of the number of clusters. PLoS ONE **11**(3), e0152333 (2016). https://doi.org/10.1371/journal.pone.0152333

27. Castro, G.F.: Modelo para el aseguramiento de ingresos en organizaciones orientadas a proyectos basado en minería de datos anómalos. Tesis de Doctorado en Ciencias Técnicas, Universidad de las Ciencias Informáticas, La Habana, Cuba (2017)

28. Shapiro, S.S., Wilk, M.B.: An analysis of variance test for normality (complete samples). Biometrika 52(3–4), 591–611 (1965). https://doi.org/10.1093/biomet/52.3-4.591

29. Wilcoxon, F., Katti, S.K., Wilcox, R.A.: Critical values and probability levels for the Wilcoxon rank sum test and the Wilcoxon signed rank test. Inst. Math. Stat. Sel. Tables Math. Stat. 1, 171–259 (1973)

30. Merigó, José M., Yager, Ronald R.: Norm aggregations and OWA operators. In: Bustince, Humberto, Fernandez, Javier, Mesiar, Radko, Calvo, Tomasa (eds.) Aggregation Functions in Theory and in Practise. AISC, vol. 228, pp. 141–151. Springer, Heidelberg (2013). https://doi.org/10.1007/978-3-642-39165-1_17

31. Piñero, P., Lugo J.A., Menéndez J., et al.: Solución de software Xedro-GESPRO v13.05. Centro Nacional de Registro de Derecho de Autor de Cuba, No Registro CENDA: 2336-06-2015, La Habana, Cuba (2015)

32. Castro, Gilberto Fernando, et al.: Platform for project evaluation based on soft-computing techniques. In: Valencia-García, Rafael, Lagos-Ortiz, Katty, Alcaraz-Mármol, Gema, del Cioppo, Javier, Vera-Lucio, Nestor (eds.) CITI 2016. CCIS, vol. 658, pp. 226–240. Springer, Cham (2016). https://doi.org/10.1007/978-3-319-48024-4_18

PID and Fuzzy Logic Controllers for DC Motor Speed Control

Eduardo Flores-Morán[1(✉)], Wendy Yánez-Pazmiño[1,2],
Luis Espin-Pazmiño[1], María Molina-Miranda[1],
and Carlos Guzmán-Real[1]

[1] Facultad de Ciencias Matemáticas y Físicas, University of Guayaquil,
Cdla. Salvador Allende, Av. Delta y Av. Kennedy, Casilla Postal 471,
Guayaquil, Ecuador
manuel.floresmo@ug.edu.ec

[2] Escuela Superior Politécnica del Litoral, ESPOL, Facultad de Ingeniería en
Electricidad y Computación, ESPOL Polytechnic University, Campus Gustavo
Galindo Km 30.5 Vía Perimetral, P.O. Box 09-01-5863, Guayaquil, Ecuador

Abstract. Proportional, integral and derivative (PID) controllers are commonly applied in industrial environments because of their performance and simplicity application in linear systems. On the other hand, Fuzzy logic controllers (FLC) imitate the human knowledge applying a linguistic ideology instead of mathematical calculations. These features make FLC suitable for nonlinear systems by providing an affordable response in terms of speed control. This research proposes a comparative study between PID controller and FLC for separately excited DC motor. Both controllers are tested under different conditions such as overshoot percentage, rise time, torque load disturbance and multiple steps input. Furthermore, this study determines the benefits and drawbacks of each controller when they are evaluated to obtain an appropriated output for DC motor speed control.

Keywords: DC motor · Fuzzy logic controller · PID controller · Speed control

1 Introduction

Separately excited DC motors transform electrical energy into mechanical energy and consist of electric-mechanical components. This type of DC motors maintains an intrinsic relation between torque and speed which has benefited its use and application in industrial processes such as trains, position system and robot arms [1].

Researchers have developed various control system methodologies to obtain an appropriated output for DC motor speed control. In this regard, PID controllers offer a feedback loop mechanism to tune their coefficients and provide an appropriate response for linear systems. Although this controller is well-known in industrial applications and applied in other systems that require module control adaptation, its application is not suitable when torque load increases [2].

© Springer Nature Switzerland AG 2019
M. Botto-Tobar et al. (Eds.): ICCCE 2018, CCIS 959, pp. 155–168, 2019.
https://doi.org/10.1007/978-3-030-12018-4_12

On the other hand, Fuzzy Logic Controller (FLC) imitates the human understanding to provide an optimal response evading mathematical calculation for linguistic ideology. This controller expresses the inputs in terms of logical variables which could be easily translated in control design. The interpretation of continuous values provides an appropriate output signal regarding to system requirements. In particular, FLC offers advantages for higher order systems and facilitates continuous parameters modification [2, 3].

Although previous works apply PID and FLC controllers for separately excited DC motors in an individual manner [2, 3], this research proposes a comparative study between these controllers. PID and FLC are tested for parameters such as torque load rejection and percentage overshoot to determine the benefits and drawbacks of each controller to obtain an appropriated output for DC motors.

The remainder of this paper is organized as follows. Section 2 provide background about DC motor, PID controllers and different methods to determine the coefficients for calculating DC motor speed control. The simulations and results of the performance of the controllers are described in Sect. 3. Section 4 summarizes the conclusions of this paper.

2 Background

2.1 DC Motor

DC motor separately excited presents two distinctive sections known as field and armature as illustrated in Fig. 1. The magnetic field is generated in the field section, while, in the armature field, an armature current (Ia) is produced by a voltage (Va) in order to generate an electro-mechanical force (E). The electro-mechanical force is related to the angular velocity (ω), and this physical phenomenon is the purpose of motors.

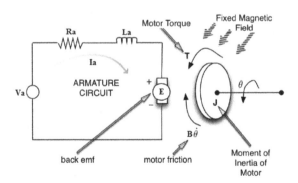

Fig. 1. Structure of DC motor.

The DC motor equations are:

$$V_a = R_a.i_a + L_a.\frac{di_a}{dt} + E \tag{1}$$

$$E = K_e.\omega.\phi \tag{2}$$

$$T_e = K_T.i_a.\phi \tag{3}$$

$$T_e = T_L + J\dot{\omega} + B\omega \tag{4}$$

Where, Ra is armature resistance in [Ω], La is armature inductance in [H], T_E is electro-mechanic torque in [N.m], T_L is torque load in [N.m], J is momentum of inertia in [Kg/m^2], B is coefficient of friction in [N.m.s], K_T is torque motor gain in [N.m/A], K_E is back electro-mechanical force coefficient in [V.s/rad], ω is angular speed in [rad/s] and φ is the flux in [Wb].

By applying Laplace transforms to the Eqs. (1), (2), (3) and (4), it is possible to elaborate a Simulink model to obtain a DC motor representation.

$$V_A(S) = R_A I_A + L_A I_A S + E(S) \tag{5}$$

$$T_E = T_L + J\dot{\omega}(S)S + B\omega(S) \tag{6}$$

From Eqs. (5) and (6), the angular speed transfer function is calculated as follows:

$$\frac{\omega(S)}{E(S)} = \frac{K}{JL_A S^2 + (JR_A + BL_A)S + (BR_A + K)} \tag{7}$$

2.2 PID Controllers

PID controllers have been implemented in more than 90% of the industrial applications and processes because of its robust performance and simplicity of parameters [4, 12]. Specifically, these controllers consist of three components: proportional (K_P), integrative (K_I) and derivative (K_D) variables. Proportional gain defines the response to the present error ($e(t)$), which corresponds to the difference between the reference and the response. By accumulating the recent errors, integrative coefficient designs the optimal responses. Derivative coefficients assign the action based on the rate at which the error has been changed [1, 4]. According to some specific parameters, PID controllers provides a control variable ($u(t)$) by adjusting their gains, in order to obtain an output signal. The structure of a PID controller is described in Fig. 2.

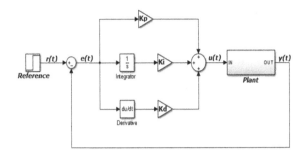

Fig. 2. Structure of PID controller.

The structure of this controller is represented by the following equation:

$$u(t) = \left[K_P.e(t) + K_I \int_0^t e(t)d\tau + K_D \frac{de(t)}{dt} \right] \tag{8}$$

Different methods could be employed to find the coefficients, such as: Ziegler-Nichols open loop response technique, closed loop or resonance technique and manual tuning.

2.3 Ziegler-Nichols Open Loop Method

Ziegler-Nichols open loop method has been implemented to acquire the PI and PID coefficients. These two types of controllers are widely applied in different industrial processes [5, 6]. By sketching a tangent line in the open loop step response, it is possible to obtain the following parameters: gain in steady-state (K), delay time (L) and time constant (T); Fig. 3 provides an overview of this process.

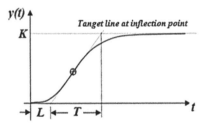

Fig. 3. Response for open loop methodology.

By applying the equation, $A = (K.L)/T$, it could obtain the PID gains through the Table 1.

Table 1. Open loop table parameters.

Controllers types	K_P	K_I	K_D
P	T/L		
PI	0.9T/L	L/0.3	
PID	1.2T/L	2L	0.5L

2.4   Ziegler-Nichols Closed Loop Resonance Method

This method initiates by setting integral and derivative coefficients to zero. The next step corresponds to increase the proportional coefficient from zero to a gain (Ku), where the step response shows a continuous oscillation [5, 6]. Finally, the response period (Tu) could be determined by measuring the time length of one cycle. Figure 4 shows this method and its parameters.

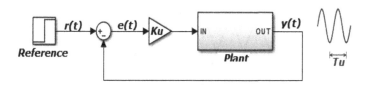

Fig. 4.   Closed loop response methodology.

The Table 2 provides the values to obtain PID gains as follow:

Table 2.   Close loop resonance table parameters.

Controllers types	K_P	K_I	K_D
P	$0.5\ K_u$		
PI	$0.4\ K_u$	$0.8\ T_u$	
PID	$0.6\ K_u$	$0.5\ T_u$	$0.125\ T_u$

Manual tuning is another alternative method to find PID coefficients, providing an output signal more affordable related to system requirements [2]. For industrial locations, a significant amount of processes or applications are determined for high order or nonlinearity systems. PID controllers operates effectively for first and second order linear systems. However, these controllers could be affected by load torque increasing or components physical deterioration. To provide a different methodology, scientist have established a technique to attend to complex systems.

2.5   Fuzzy Logic Controller

In 1965, Dr. Lotfi A. Zadeh established the concept of Fuzzy logic controller to deal with known drawbacks of PID controllers. FLC is able to control complex systems by executing a linguistic ideology achieved from the experience and knowledge of the operator [7, 8]. This controller offers a procedure for symbolizing and applying an interpretation of programmer experience, in order to establish a signal that works over the plant. Fuzzifier, knowledge base, inference mechanism and defuzzifier are the FLC components, where $e(t)$ is the error, $ce(t)$ is the change of error and $u(t)$ is the control variable.

Fuzzifier. This component transforms a standardized input gain into an etymological term. For example, it is able to obtain an exemplification as negative small (NS) or big positive (BP) by estimating the membership function. The most used shape is triangular waveform. Figure 5 shows a general idea of this component.

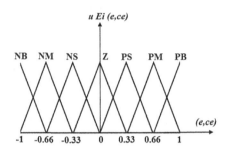

Fig. 5. Example of the membership function of $e(t)$ and $ce(t)$.

Knowledge Base. This module offers the database and rules for the FLC. Knowledge base is the responsible component for providing information to all FLC elements. Rule base consists of a set of linguistic interpretation related to the input and the desired output.

Inference Mechanism. Inference process defines the FLC output by calculating the knowledge base commands. The programmer skill or knowledge establish the commands that offer the output values, for example:

If $e(t)$ is Em and $ce(t)$ is dEn then $f(t)$ is Cmn.

Where the functions incomes are defined by Em and dEn, $f(t)$ corresponds to the controller output and Cmn is the output function.

Defuzzifier. In this section, FLC output is transformed into numerical gain. There are different types of defuzzifiers such as mean of maximum, center of gravity, center of average.

PD, PI and PD + I are the most applied FLC schematic. The well-known drawbacks of the FLC correspond to elaborate the scheme of the rules, select the fitting defuzzi-fier and find an appropriate response [8, 9, 11].

3   Simulation and Results

Matlab/Simulink offers a valuable software tool to study the performance of the controllers. This section analyzes the behavior for speed control of a separately excited DC motor tuned by (1) open, (2) closed loop methodology, (3) manual tuning and (4) Fuzzy PD + I controllers. These methods are evaluated under different factors such as disturbance rejecting and multiple steps input.

For the first section of this examination, 1000 rad/s step input is applied to each controller. Table 3 shows the DC motor parameters for the simulation.

Table 3. DC motor parameters.

Parameters	Value
R_a	2.45 [Ω]
L_a	0.035 [H]
J	0.022 [Kg/m^2]
B	0.0005 [N.m.s]
K_E	1.2 [V.s/rad]
K_T	1.2 [N.m/A]

Applying the Eq. 7, angular speed transfer function is shown as follows:

$$\frac{\omega(S)}{E(S)} = \frac{1558.4}{S^2 + 70.02S + 1872} \tag{9}$$

Method 1: Ziegler Nichols Open Loop Response
Ziegler Nichols open loop response provides a quick methodology to find the PID parameters – A and L. By applying a step response to the DC motor, the value of these variables is 0.0286 and 0.0375 respectively. For this study, PID configuration is used due to its robustness. Table 4 shows the PID gains and Fig. 6 displays the step response for PID controller. The percentage overshoot is 12.4% and rise time is 0.0315 s.

Table 4. PID coefficients obtained by open loop response methodology.

Controllers types	K_P	K_I	K_D
P	34.96		
PI	31.47	279.7	
PID	41.96	559.5	0.79

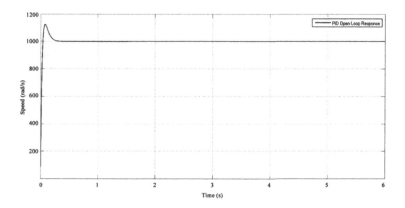

Fig. 6. Step response for PID controller tuned by open loop methodology.

Method 2: Ziegler Nichols Closed Loop Response

This methodology is essential to calculate the parameters Ku and Tu whose values are 75 and 0.5 respectively. The coefficients of these controllers are shown in Table 5. For this examination, PID controller is the most suitable to be applied due to its effectiveness and efficient. Figure 7 shows the step response, obtaining a percentage overshoot of 12% and rise time of 0.105 s.

Table 5. PID coefficients obtained by closed loop response methodology.

Controllers types	K_P	K_I	K_D
P	42.1		
PI	33.68	290.3	
PID	50.52	696.8	0.92

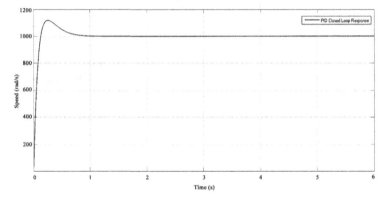

Fig. 7. Step response for PID controller tuned by closed loop.

Method 3: Manual Tuning

For PID controller tuned by manual adjusting, Table 6 shows its gains and Fig. 8 displays the step response. The overshoot percentage and rise time are 0% and 0.104 s, respectively. As a previous methodology, PID controller provides an optimal response for the requirements specification.

Table 6. PID coefficients obtained by manual tuning.

Controllers type	K_P	K_I	K_D
PID	2.2	23	0.05

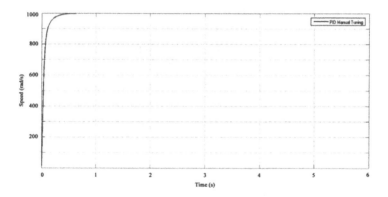

Fig. 8. Step response for PID controller tuned by manual adjusting.

Method 4: Fuzzy PD + I

According to the aforementioned explanation, FLC offers a feasible solution for non-linear systems by executing an etymological philosophy, avoiding any calculation, in order to define the action of system control variable [10, 11]. For this examination, the two inputs of the fuzzy PD + I controller are error and change of error, and the output works over the system.

By a trial and error methodology, it is possible to obtain the membership functions of the FLC, related to the system requirements [2, 10]. The membership functions of the Fuzzy PD + I controller are shown in the Fig. 9.

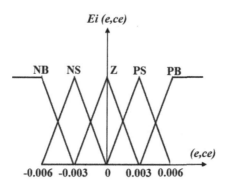

Fig. 9. Error, change of error and output membership functions for Fuzzy PD + I controller.

Table 7 shows 25 fuzzy rules which can be established by the observation and testing of the system performance. Table 8 displays the fuzzy PD + I gains of the system.

Table 7. FLC rules.

	NB	NS	Z	PS	PB
PB	Z	PS	PB	PB	PB
PS	NS	Z	PS	PB	PB
Z	NB	NS	Z	PS	PB
NS	NB	NB	NS	Z	PS
NB	NB	NB	NB	NS	Z

Table 8. Fuzzy PD + I Coefficients.

Parameters	Value
K_E	0.7
K_{CE}	0.05
K_U	1.1
K_I	8

Figure 10 displays the step response for Fuzzy PD + I controller, the percentage overshoot is 0% and rise time is 0.291 s. This response is produced because the integral term acts as an accumulator of the previous error.

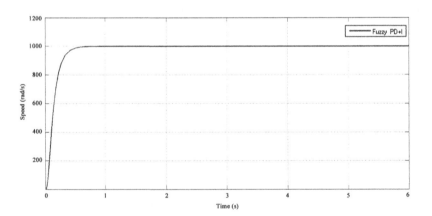

Fig. 10. Step response for Fuzzy PD + I controller.

This study contains an examination of variable steps input. The multiple input initiates at 1000 rad/s; at 2 s, the reference growths to 1200 rad/s. At the end, the input decreases to 800 rad/s at 4 s. The Fig. 11 displays the responses for the three controllers. For multiple steps inputs, the behavior of each controller maintains its performance. Ziegler Nichols open and closed loop response offer an output signal with a significant overshoot (over 12%). This effect is produced due the proportional and integral action. In contrast, manual tuning provides a response without overshoot because its integral coefficient is considerable small. Figure 12 shows the responses for Fuzzy PD + I controller.

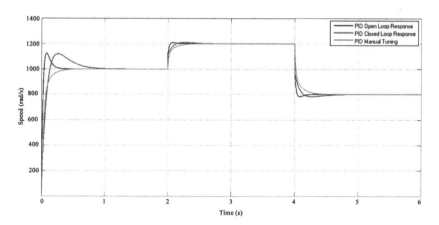

Fig. 11. Multiple steps response for PID controllers.

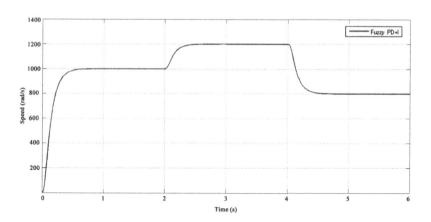

Fig. 12. Multiple steps response for Fuzzy PD + I.

At 3 s, a 5% torque load disturbance is executed to the DC motor, for open loop response methodology PID controller response drops to 998.1 rad/s and the time that takes to return to the reference point is 0.21 s. For closed loop methodology, the response decays to 998.3 rad/s and the time to recover the reference is 0.62 s. For manual tuning, the output signal drops to 973.5 rad/s and the time to recover the reference is 0.63 s. Figure 13 shows the torque load rejection for PID controllers. Basically, this time can be eliminated by growing the integral term, however, this effects produce a rise of the overshoot percentage. According to Fuzzy PD + I, the response drops to 925 rad/s. As demonstrated in the preceding examination, Fuzzy PD + I presents a slow performance because the integral gain works as sum of the output before to it. FLC's linguistic representation offers a methodology to eliminate complex calculations. Figure 14 displays the disturbance rejection for Fuzzy PD + I controllers.

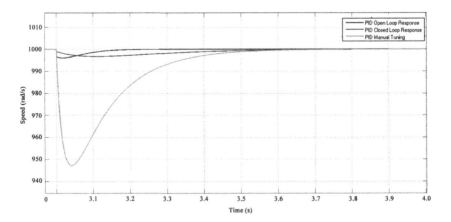

Fig. 13. Torque load rejection for PID controllers.

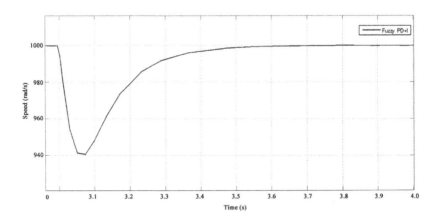

Fig. 14. Torque load rejection for Fuzzy PD + I controller.

4   Conclusion

This paper aims to obtain an appropriated output for separately excited DC motor by comparing different control methodologies including PID controllers and FLC. These controllers have been tested under different conditions such as overshoot percentage, rise time, torque load disturbance and multiple steps input. According to the results, Ziegler Nichols approach provides an output with a considerable overshoot percentage and a slow torque load rejection. On the other hand, PID controller tuned by manual adjusting shows a reduction in proportional and integral terms which in turn produces an output response without overshoot and an appropriated torque load rejection. In the case of FLC, the output response does not present an overshoot and acceptable torque load rejection, but the response is slow since the integral term act as an accumulator of the previous error. To summarize, PID controller tuned by manual adjusting seems to be the most appropriated scheme for DC motor speed control based on the above described parameters. As a future study, the efficient of the proposed controller can be analyzed and compared with an optimizer.

References

1. Tipsuwanporn, V., Numsomran, A., Klinsmitth, N., Gulphanich, S.: Separately excited DC motor drive with fuzzy self-organizing. In: 2007 International Conference on Control, Automation and Systems, Seoul, pp. 1316–1321 (2007)
2. Morán, M.E.F., Viera, N.A.P.: Comparative study for DC motor position controllers. In: 2017 IEEE Second Ecuador Technical Chapters Meeting (ETCM), pp. 1–6 (2017)
3. Arrofiq, M., Saad, N.: A simulation of PLC-based self-tuning PI - fuzzy logic controller for DC motor. In: 2008 International Symposium on Information Technology, Kuala Lumpur, Malaysia, pp. 1–8 (2008)
4. Dani, S., Sonawane, D., Ingole, D., Patil, S.: Performance evaluation of PID, LQR and MPC for DC motor speed control. In: 2017 2nd International Conference for Convergence in Technology (I2CT), Mumbai, pp. 348–354 (2017)
5. Kukolj, D., Kulic, F., Levi, E.: Artificial intelligence based gain scheduling of PI speed controller in DC motor drives. In: Proceedings of the IEEE International Symposium on Industrial Electronics. ISIE 1999, Bled, pp. 425–429 (1999)
6. Muñoz-César, J.J., Merchán-Cruz, E.A., Hernández-Gómez, L.H., Guerrero-Guadarrama, E., Jiménez-Ledesma, A., Jaidar-Monter, I.: Speed control of a DC brush motor with conventional PID and fuzzy PI controllers. In: Electronics, Robotics and Automotive Mechanics Conference. CERMA 2008, Morelos, pp. 344–349 (2008)
7. Ghalehpardaz, S.L., Shafiee, M.: Speed control of DC motor using imperialist competitive algorithm based on PI-Like FLC. In: 2011 Third International Conference on Computational Intelligence, Modelling & Simulation, Langkawi, pp. 28–33 (2011)
8. Almutairi, N.B., Chow, M.Y.: A modified PI control action with a robust adaptive fuzzy controller applied to DC motor. In: Proceedings of the International Joint Conference on Neural Networks. IJCNN 2001. Washington, DC, pp. 503–508 (2001)
9. Gupta, S.K., Varshney, P.: Fractional fuzzy PID controller for speed control of DC motor. In: 2013 Third International Conference on Advances in Computing and Communications, Cochin, pp. 1–4 (2013)
10. Sahputro, S.D., Fadilah, F., Wicaksono, N.A., Yusivar, F.: Design and implementation of adaptive PID controller for speed control of DC motor. In: 2017 15th International Conference on Quality in Research (QiR): International Symposium on Electrical and Computer Engineering, Nusa Dua, pp. 179–183 (2017)

11. Flores-Morán, E., Yánez-Pazmiño, W., Barzola-Monteses, J.: Genetic algorithm and fuzzy self-tuning PID for DC motor position controllers. In: 2018 19th International Carpathian Control Conference (ICCC), Szilvasvarad, pp. 162–168 (2018)
12. Haz, L., Calle, W., Moran, M.E.F., Carcelen, J., Cortez, A., Nunez-Unda, A.: Design of smart stretchers and vital signs monitoring system for reduced-mobility patients. In: 2018 13th Iberian Conference on Information Systems and Technologies (CISTI), Caceres, pp. 1–5 (2018)

Author Index

Printed in the United States
By Bookmasters